THE

REFERENCE

SHELF

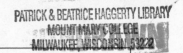
THE HOMELESS PROBLEM

Edited by MATTHEW A. KRALJIC

THE REFERENCE SHELF

Volume 64, Number 2

THE H. W. WILSON COMPANY

New York   1992

THE REFERENCE SHELF

The books in this series contain reprints of articles, excerpts from books, and addresses on current issues and social trends in the United States and other countries. There are six separately bound numbers in each volume, all of which are generally published in the same calendar year. One number is a collection of recent speeches; each of the others is devoted to a single subject and gives background information and discussion from various points of view, concluding with a comprehensive bibliography that contains books and pamphlets and abstracts of additional articles on the subject. Books in the series may be purchased individually or on subscription.

Library of Congress Cataloging-in-Publication Data

The Homeless problem / edited by Matthew A. Kraljic.
    p.   cm. — (The Reference shelf ; v. 64, no. 2)
  Includes bibliographical references.
  ISBN 0-8242-0826-9
  1. Homelessness—United States.   I. Kraljic, Matthew A.
II. Series.
HV4505.H6552   1992
362.5'8'0973—dc20   92-5909
                                                         CIP

Cover: A Homeless person sleeps in a New York City doorway.
Photo: Lee Snider/Photo Images

Printed in the United States of America

CONTENTS

PREFACE

Along with food, health, and personal safety, there is probably no greater basic need for human beings than shelter. Indeed, aside from loss of these other three fundamental necessities, nothing is more likely to scar the psyche and soul of an individual than homelessness. For many in society, the prospect of homelessness is perhaps the most frightening of societal ills because it tends to be the most visible. When the public housing projects and shelters are filled, homelessness spills over onto the streets and stares us in the face, a hand extended in a plea for help—for what spare change you can offer.

When first confronted by this vision, few can be unmoved. It is, however, when the homeless become too difficult to view, the problem too overwhelming to comprehend, or the implications (there but for the grace of God . . .) too threatening to bear that we often develop a protective, or defensive, blind spot to the disease. Most appalling is the knowledge that homelessness is often the harbinger, if not the catalyst, of hunger, sickness, and peril. Life on the streets is one spent facing countless dangers. A person without a home is a victim many times over in a society where apathy so often seems to replace compassion and lip service substitutes for action.

Section One of this compilation begins by examining efforts to quantify and qualify the problem of homelessness. Some of the commentators doubt there really is such a problem in the United States. Others question its severity, using 1990 U.S. Census Bureau data and its reliability as a focal point, while raising questions of individual and social responsibility.

Section Two presents articles that move the image from the abstract to the concrete and individual. Although a significant number of the homeless people fit traditional stereotypes of the skid row bum (a victim of alcoholism or substance addiction) and the displaced mental patient, a significant number of today's homeless are in fact former members of the middle class who have become economically disenfranchised by shifts in the American workplace and its financial institutions. A disproportionate number are children—both as members of intact and single-parent families living on the streets, and as teenage runaways. No

7

longer a solely urban problem, homelessness has begun to tax the resources and patience of suburban and rural communities, too.

The articles in Section Three focus on some of the main causes of the homeless problem. Part of the problem stems from decades of urban renewal which created parking lots, high-rise buildings, and gentrified neighborhoods in place of affordable housing, the preservation of which many communities seemed unwilling to underwrite. Then there is the scarcity of psychiatric and medical health care programs to handle the mentally deficient, the psychologically addicted, and the physically ill. Added to these factors is the economic imbalance of the past decade affecting those at the bottom of trickle-down economic models.

In 1954, at the height of the post-war economic boom, the American educator Robert Maynard Hutchins wrote, "The death of democracy is not likely to be an assassination from ambush. It will be a slow extinction from apathy, indifference, and undernourishment." As if to prove his speculation true, governmental efforts to solve the problem, especially at the federal level, have so far been anemic and ineffective, while overall public sentiment toward the homeless seem to range from apathy to hostility. Section Four, however, provides articles that explore what may work to alleviate at least some of the suffering of the homeless. By examining programs that combine volunteerism, private sector aid, and public policy initiatives, this final sampling of articles points to a range of possible philosophies and strategies that may enable society to grapple more realistically and more successfully with the problem of homelessness.

The editor is indebted to the authors and publishers who have granted permission for these materials to be reprinted herein. In addition, special thanks are due to the reference staff of the Patchogue Public Library, and to my wife and family for their patience and understanding.

MATTHEW A. KRALJIC

December 1991

I. THE NUMBERS GAME

EDITOR'S INTRODUCTION

As with most issues that concern dividing up the social welfare pot, the first question that policy planners ask when addressing the problem of homelessness is, how much of a problem is it? Although the 1990 U.S. Census is the source most government aid programs rely upon, the methods used for gathering its statistics have been called into question. In addition, other studies, often funded, sponsored, or conducted by groups with their own political agendas, draw similar fire from skeptics and those displeased with their findings. The first article in this section, by Ed Rubenstein of the *National Review* looks at the implications of believing in one or another set of statistics on the homeless. In addition, the author's brief analysis of the relationship between housing and homelessness suggest a view of where some solutions might lie.

Next, reviewing the controversy of which the numbers dilemma is only a part, Michael Levitas, writing in *The New York Times Magazine,* reflects on disagreements over who the homeless are and how they came to become homeless. The importance of these questions should not be underestimated as public willingness to support those fallen on hard economic times through a spate of bad luck would more than likely be significantly different from the willingness to support a so-called skid row bum. The article also delves into the semantics of defining homelessness, which is a part of the struggle among interest groups fighting over pieces of the public budget pie. While consensus seems to exist in identifying lack of affordable housing as a culprit in the overall homeless problem, opinion is divided over the availability of federal funds to address the issue. Although social spending had in the past been effective in all but erradicating poverty among the elderly by large-scale spending on social security, the article concludes by questioning whether enough money does or will exist any time soon to effectively turn the tide of homelessness in the United States.

Finally, Charles E. King writing in *The Humanist* suggests that

our resolve to recognize and meet the obligations of an affluent
society to help its members in need in part of a basic social contract in which "if we accept the benefits of the system, we must
accept the responsibilities."

RIGHT DATA: HOW MANY HOMELESS?[1]

Advocates for the homeless are understandably annoyed at
"shelter night," the Census Bureau's well-publicized effort to
count the homeless population. For years these groups have
traded on the figure of three million homeless—1.2 per cent of
the nation's population. The media generally report this figure.
Politicians and celebrities cite it. Yet every systematic survey of
homelessness since 1984 has put the figure at between 250,000
and 600,000, with the average at about 400,000. The only study
to reach a seven-figure estimate, *Homelessness: A Forced March to
Nowhere,* was published by activist Mitch Snyder in 1982, and was
based on a phone survey of shelter operators across the country.

The tricky part of any attempt to count the homeless is to
determine the ratio of street homeless to shelter homeless. We
know there are approximately 275,000 beds in shelters throughout the country. A HUD survey conducted in January 1984 found
only 70 per cent of shelter beds occupied. Even assuming full
occupancy, and even defining each of the approximately 110,000
persons in public mental hospitals as "homeless," the street-to-
shelter ratio would have to be 8 to 1 for there to be three million
homeless. Advocates for the homeless insist that street people go
to great lengths to hide themselves and are grossly undercounted,
but most studies have found the average annual street-to-shelter
ratio to be less than 1 to 1, far less in those cities, such as New
York, where shelters are readily available.

Researchers generally agree that between 35 and 40 per cent
of homeless individuals have severe drug or alcohol problems,
and 50 per cent are disabled by mental illness. A 1988 Urban
Institute study was the first to look at other characteristics, and

[1]Article by Ed Rubenstein, from *National Review* 42:17 My 14 '90. Copyright ©
1990 by *National Review,* Inc., 150 East 35th Street, New York, NY 10016. Reprinted
by permission.

found that 56 per cent had served five or more days in jail, while more than 25 per cent had served time in state or federal prisons, implying felony convictions. Almost 50 per cent never finished high school, and only 5 per cent had steady employment. This contrasts sharply with the image portrayed by the media: the Center for Media and Public Affairs reports that only 12 per cent of the homeless interviewed for the three networks' evening news shows were unemployed, and only 3 per cent were drug or alcohol users. Their survey covered 103 stories on homelessness broadcast over a thirty-month period.

To what extent, then, is homelessness strictly a housing problem? We might start with the 10 per cent of homeless households made up of families with children. These families are poor, but relatively few members are drug addicts or mentally ill. However, most of these families are headed by females—half of them never married—suggesting that even in this group few are homeless solely because of a lack of affordable housing.

In New York City an average of 12,000 families are homeless over the course of a year. Surely the city's housing supply—1.9 million rental units—could be stretched to accommodate a less than 1 per cent rise in inhabitants. Where rents are not controlled this is accomplished by means of upward migration: affluent tenants move to better apartments, their old units are acquired by those just below them on the housing ladder, eventually freeing up the least desirable units for the poor and homeless. But one of the strictest rent-control laws in the nation induces New Yorkers to hold onto their apartments long after their incomes have risen, their families have grown, and, in many cases, they themselves have left town.

HOMELESS IN AMERICA[2]

One of the most incongruous snapshots of America's homeless men and women can be taken daily at about 4:30 in the

[2]Article by Mitchel Levitas, senior editor of *The New York Times*, from *The New York Times Magazine* 140:45+ Je 10 '90. Copyright © 1990 by The New York Times Company. Reprinted with permission.

afternoon on one of the two large lawns that flank the entrance to
City Hall on Main Street in Santa Monica, Calif. The neatly
trimmed grass, the blue canopy and Art Deco mosaic tiles over
the front doors of the white, two-story building just two blocks
from the serene Pacific, is an odd setting for a soup kitchen.
Private volunteers of Family Assistance Involving the Homeless,
or Faith, serve 250 or 300 people a hot supper and dessert. Several park rangers stand around in case of trouble, but on this sunny,
cool afternoon the line moves quietly along the perimeter of
bright green grass toward the tables of food. Wearing down jackets and windbreakers (one or two men are in suits) and carrying
knapsacks, duffel bags or black plastic garbage bags, the homeless
seem mostly in their 20's or 30's; some are black, some white; men
far outnumber women. A middle-aged street woman dressed in
layers of clothing feeds her toy poodle vegetables with a teaspoon;
its doghouse is a mobile home—a carton wedged at the front of a
shopping cart piled high with possessions.

    The scene is familiar to Barbara Stinchfield, the community
development manager of this prosperous city of 90,000 whose
liberal politics have inspired conservatives to call it the People's
Republic of Santa Monica. [In 1985,] . . . Stinchfield said: "Our
homeless task force had a very positive feeling, trying to address
the problems of a few hundred veterans and families, single men
and women. We won awards for an innovative outreach program
and a day center for mentally ill women. Then the numbers of
homeless got so great"—about a thousand is the highest estimate—"that people thought, 'My God, we're going under!' Now
we feel like desperate people in a desperate city."

    Across Main Street from City Hall, along a landscaped knoll
that overlooks Faith's food line, is the low-rise glass headquarters
of the Rand Corporation, where cadres of hands-on analysts are
employed to think deeply about solutions to vital problems facing
the United States in peace and war. [In 1987,] . . . Rand got into
the homeless question. Under a new five-year, $2.3 million grant
from the National Institute of Mental Health, Audrey Burnam of
Rand and Paul Koegel of the University of California at Los Angeles are trying to learn how mentally ill homeless people in Santa
Monica and on Skid Row in Los Angeles manage to find a home,
or at least a roof over their heads, as most of them do after less
than a year on the street. "We don't understand why and how
they cease to become homeless," says Burnam. "Where do they
go? How does that happen? What kind of housing is useful and
what support services do they really need?"

The Rand study may clarify some of the many uncertainties still surrounding the homeless population. The basic questions begin with its size and composition. Is the number of homeless about 600,000 on any given day, as the Urban Institute, a non-profit research organization in Washington, believes? Or is it closer to the 3 million claimed by advocates for the homeless? Even harder to agree on are the causes and strategies for attacking the phenomenon. Whatever the answers, the fact that Rand has turned its attention to this issue suggests that homelessness may well have become a permanent feature of poverty in America.

It has all happened in less than a decade, after the experts realized that the 1981–82 recession was not a temporary spasm, but an early warning of an evolving, major socioeconomic breakdown. *Homeless*—a word that until recently was virtually unknown in the public-policy vocabulary—has become a slogan, a stigma and a symbol of the country's reluctance and inability to relieve a novel suffering among its poorest people.

As President-elect, George Bush called homelessness a "national shame." Jack Kemp, Secretary of Housing and Urban Development, likes to call himself "a bleeding heart conservative" when it comes to housing for the poor. And Anna Kondratas, H.U.D.'s assistant secretary for community planning and development, asserts that although "the problem is shocking and getting worse," she's convinced that it will be turned around in this decade. "After all," she said, "this is the land of the rich as well as the free, by world standards, and we should be able to do it."

Is this climate of rhetorical concern a sign of Federal determination to attack homelessness? Or is it really going to be up to the states and cities to find solutions—and pay for them? The trouble is, solutions depend on how homelessness is defined and who makes the definitions. Public officials? Academic experts in welfare economics or the dynamics of poverty? And what about the thousands of volunteer groups and other advocates who have so far shaped the debate and provided the services to help the homeless? Are they capable of coping with such a threatening phenomenon? In short, who is doing what about eradicating this "national shame"?

Some answers emerged in more than a month of travel to several cities, each with its own problems, and talks with dozens of scholars, advocates, service providers and public officials. One conclusion is evident: There is no grand strategy aimed at eliminating homelessness, no master blueprint on the drawing board of the social engineers. The very complexity of homelessness explains why so many partial "solutions" are inescapable. "It's the most fascinating, frustrating public policy issue I've ever been involved in," said Gordon Berlin, who . . . finished up a stint as the chief for management, policy and budget of New York City's Human Resources Agency [in 1990].

Berlin's feelings are widely shared, even by advocates who are prone to boiling down the problem to three causes, "housing, housing, housing," and three cures, "housing, housing, housing." Homelessness, as James D. Wright, a Tulane University sociologist and author of "Address Unknown," has written, is "simul- taneously a housing problem, an employment problem, a demo- graphic problem, a problem of social disaffiliation, a mental health problem, a family violence problem, a problem created by the cutbacks in social welfare spending, a problem resulting from the decay of the traditional nuclear family, and a problem inti- mately connected to the recent increase in the number of persons living below the poverty level."

Even that partial list of targets makes the 1960's War on Pover- ty seem like a simple commando raid. Lyndon B. Johnson pre- sided during a period of moral fervor over civil rights, coupled with Great Society domestic spending. In today's climate, said Wright: "The solutions are almost prohibitive. Moreover, there doesn't seem to be an entry point into the problem because every subgroup in the homeless"—single young men, single women, one-parent families, alcoholics, families in which no one is em- ployed, the mentally ill, the elderly—"has its own complex of needs. The drug problem is getting worse all the time." "And," he summed up, "I think in all honesty that we're losing ground. The 1990's will be worse than the 1980's."

Not everyone is as pessimistic, but few activists or social ser- vice providers are optimistic either. In what many argue is an abdication of Federal responsibility, thousands of advocates and volunteer groups have had to learn new organizing skills, patch- ing together funds from half a dozen sources while avoiding the snares of bureaucracy. Their many successes come in small victo- ries—the neighborhood, not the nation, is their focus. The law- yer-advocates are more politically savvy, and look a little further down the road. Gary Blasi is a housing lawyer in Los Angeles who specialized in fighting evictions, which is how he began defending the homeless and wound up as president of the National Coalition for the Homeless; his term was recently extended, he reported without enthusiasm. Blasi isn't weary, exactly. It's just that he knows the score.

"If God stopped the creation of homeless people," he said, "we might, with enormous expense and effort, get back to normal within two or three years. But we still will need fewer poor people or more cheap housing. Otherwise, the process will go on forever. That's why the energy of the advocates goes for housing and raising incomes. We can't solve this problem on the basis of humanitarianism. Thank God for saints and martyrs, but the problem goes well beyond that.

"The future? The pessimist in me sees homelessness becoming a permanent part of American society, with millions of kids growing up in an essentially third-world country with all those sadly familiar extremes of wealth and poverty. The other possibility is that people will decide it's curable and fix it. It's a question of political priorities and public perception."

About a million flophouse rooms have been torn down nationwide since the 1970's, when cities across the land began to rejuvenate their downtowns. Bowery bums who worked occasionally are among today's homeless.

What's left of Skid Row in Los Angeles says a lot about the homeless problem. The 55 square blocks just east of the spiffy new downtown is the scene of intensive rescue and renewal aimed at 11,000 Skid Row men and women who live in the 65 remaining single-room-occupancy hotels, or spend the night in the 2,000 emergency beds and chairs provided by half a dozen missions; all but one of the missions provide sermons along with shelter. City shelters open only when it's raining, cold (below 40 degrees) or when the weather is threatening.

Six years ago, the city's Community Redevelopment Agency hired Andy Raubeson from a successful S.R.O. program in Portland, Ore., to do the same in Los Angeles, where the homeless population is usually estimated at 50,000 to 70,000. The S.R.O. Housing Corporation, partly financed by a new tax base from downtown skyscrapers, opened its first renovated flophouse in 1986; the city passed a five-year moratorium on the further destruction or conversion of S.R.O.'s in 1989 (about 2,300 units were lost between 1969 and 1986), and now Raubeson's outfit owns 13 S.R.O.'s and is adding two more.

Joining the S.R.O. Housing Corporation in the race to reno-

vate is the nonprofit Skid Row Housing Trust, whose president is
Alice Callaghan, an energetic Episcopal priest and former
nun, . . . doesn't think of Skid Row as a homeless community, but
as an "endangered low-income residential community" with jobs
in fish processing and wholesale toys, and under hostile pressure
from Little Tokyo, a growing enclave of Asian commerce. Real
estate values in Skid Row are climbing 15 percent a year, evidently
in the belief that commercial growth is inexorable, moratorium or
not. The trust's first project did away with a rendezvous for drug
dealers and prostitutes, reborn in 1988 as the 29-room Genesis
Hotel, in a partnership between a Pasadena Episcopal church and
a West Los Angeles synagogue. The trust now owns 10 hotels,
three already gutted and redesigned with community kitchens,
skylights, pastel colors and cheerful tile floors. There is a manager on the premises, in case of trouble or if someone sees demons
in the middle of the night.

According to a blue-ribbon commission appointed by Mayor
Tom Bradley, one-fourth of all renters paid more than half their
income for housing, a burden that often leads to homelessness.
The average rent in Los Angeles in 1988 was $525 a month, 70
percent of the income of a minimum-wage worker, and more
than twice the rent in 1980. But during the last 20 years, the value
of welfare payments to about 4 million adults (principally Aid to
Families with Dependent Children), and other forms of welfare
assistance has declined by more than a third, making cheap, decent housing almost impossible to find. H.U.D. appropriations
for subsidized housing programs were cut by 75 percent during
the Reagan Administration, from $33 billion in 1981 to $8 billion
in 1988; about 500,000 people were dropped from the welfare
rolls after being declared ineligible.

Advocates point to numbers like these and argue that Washington is responsible for the sudden appearance of homelessness
in the 1980's. Anna Kondratas of H.U.D. rejects the idea that
Federal policies are the root cause of the problem; it thus follows,
in her view, that Federal policies are not the root solutions either.
Similarly, Stuart M. Butler, director of domestic-policy studies at
the Heritage Foundation, a conservative think tank, believes that
more housing only ignores "the disabilities" among the "majority"
of the homeless: "either mental illness, long-term drug and alcohol abuse, or a combination of the two."

John P. Singleton, vice chairman of Los Angeles's Security
Pacific Corporation, heads an $8 million drive for a new home for
the 99-year-old Union Rescue Mission. Like Butler, he believes

that "government aggravates the problem, not solves it." But Singleton concedes that volunteerism has its limits: "We were ready to spend $100 million to keep the Raiders in town. Where is our sense of priorities?"

A few miles down the Santa Monica Freeway, Vivian Rothstein asked the same question. Her Ocean Park Community Center raises $800,000 a year from private sources, "but there is no way the nonprofits can meet the needs of the homeless," she said. "The Feds have walked off the scene. We're literally keeping people alive, and we were not set up for that." Goaded by such frustrations, some providers are seeking new means to end homelessness, taking hundreds of small steps at a time. Maxene Johnston has converted a dangerous 11-story fleabag hotel ("A murder a day at the old El Rey," was the local wisecrack) into the Weingart Center, which includes under one roof an inexpensive cafeteria operated by a national food service company; county medical, mental health and welfare services; 600 beds, most of them in private rooms; an alcohol detoxification unit; a Veterans Administration office, and an assortment of referral services.

Tanya Tull has been helping Los Angeles homeless for a decade, first by mobilizing emergency shelters, then by starting transitional housing programs. She recently founded two nonprofit groups that operate permanent housing with support services for the mentally ill and for families with children. "It's impossible to find enough transitional beds," she maintains. "Besides, moving people around from one place to another isn't normal. We helped create the monster of dependency. Now we have to redirect our energies and re-educate the public toward supported, independent housing."

On Skid Row, Jill Halverson runs the Downtown Women's Center and 48 units of adjoining, permanent housing. The architectural design is modern and cozy, complete with a porch light over each door and an old-fashioned mailbox to create the feeling of a home for the once-homeless mentally ill and elderly residents. "We got to know the women at the drop-in day center," Halverson explains. "So we take as tenants those who are willing to accept treatment or who can profit from it. It made sense to bite the bullet on permanent housing. After all, what do they transition to?"

People who live in Minneapolis, describing the rate of crime, addiction, poverty and family violence in the city's near North

Side, call it "our South Bronx." If the South Bronx had lawns,
decently kept one-family houses and clean streets, the com-
parison might seem more credible. Minneapolis and neighboring
St. Paul, across the Mississippi, also know homelessness, but like
other problems in the Twin Cities it almost seems manageable.

Cold winters help, discouraging heavy migration. But a combination of political liberalism, a Scandinavian and German cultural inheritance, enlightened corporations and relative pros-
perity has done much to create a sense of civic-mindedness. The
McKnight Foundation, for example, supports projects for the
state's disadvantaged; according to Tom Fulton, president of
the Minneapolis/Saint Paul Family Housing Fund, the foundation
has given his organization a total of $28 million for local low-cost
housing development. Church groups and other volunteer agencies in the Twin Cities have created more than half a dozen emergency shelters with about a thousand beds and several drop-in
centers that serve meals. On the night of Feb. 22, the shelter
population was 1,022, almost the same as last year, according to a
head count by the Wilder Foundation. Blacks are disproportion-
ately represented among the homeless in American cities; even in
metropolitan Minneapolis, which is less than 15 percent black,
blacks constituted an estimated 41 percent of the foundation's
census. (Whites were 37 percent; Hispanic people, 9 percent;
American Indian, 10 percent; Asian, 1 percent.)

Two of the most innovative programs in Minneapolis are
aimed at homeless mothers and their children, the fastest-growing component of the homeless population nationally. One program is run from a small office in a Presbyterian church by Sue
Watlov Phillips, who last year installed 138 adults and children in
suburban homes leased by her Elim Transitional Housing organization. One ranch house was a temporary refuge for four homeless women and three children: one had a violent boyfriend; another's husband had started using drugs; the parents of a third
were dealing in drugs; the fourth got pregnant and had been
thrown out by her mother.

Another program, focused directly on youngsters, is the
Learning Center, operating from cheerful quarters in the base-
ment of a former motel, now a shelter for homeless families. "It's
a place of learning and fun," Panna M. Putnam, its director, told a
dozen youngsters seated at their desks, poised to write a collective
poem. Putnam said the children are curious and bright, but building trust is difficult when the average stay at the motel is 21 days.

The women are so desperate for housing that they wind up in the same situation they were in before: bad neighborhoods, substandard housing, high rents and eviction. "It's a revolving door," said Putnam. "And within a year we see half the same families again."

"Unless we put money into permanent affordable housing," said Tom Fulton of the Family Housing Fund, "we're just dealing on an emergency basis." Doing their best to fill the need, a dozen neighborhood-based community development organizations are actively buying abandoned buildings, and constructing new ones; in the last eight years they've created 3,000 low-cost permanent housing units. J. Paul Getty's birthplace, The Heritage, on the edge of downtown Minneapolis, has been remodeled by the Central Community Housing Trust, which has finished or has under way a dozen such projects. The Heritage is now 16 units of carpeted efficiency apartments, renting to the formerly homeless for one-third of their monthly income.

With all the problem-solving energy of the Twin Cities, is homelessness declining? "The basic problems are beyond our control," replied Fulton. "When you provide more, you're helping someone. But I can't honestly say we're winning the battle, no."

After a five-year flood of crises, Gordon Berlin, a key strategist in the Human Resources Administration of former Mayor Edward I. Koch, hopes that the tide of homelessness in New York City—at least 35,000 people, and perhaps twice that number—might be getting easier to manage. Though the city [had difficulty meeting a] deadline for moving homeless families out of welfare hotels, the worst hotels have been emptied and the number has dropped sharply even though 800 new families enter the system every month. "What we've done is a miracle, and we get no credit for it," Berlin said.

The most important city effort to contain homelessness is a 10-year $5.1 billion program to construct and rebuild 84,000 new apartments by 1996. Of that total, 15,000 are earmarked for homeless families—most of them single mothers with children. In half of these cases the women never had a home of their own before, living doubled up with parents or boyfriends. Andrew Cuomo, whose Housing Enterprise for the Less Privileged organization in New York State builds transitional housing for families, has estimated that at least half the mothers and older children in his facilities have a drug problem. Seventy-five percent of the new permanent housing for homeless single mothers is in the

South Bronx, Cuomo pointed out: "We have just moved the Mar-
tinique Hotel there and built a time bomb. Unless these women
become self-supporting, society should be prepared to take care
of them and their kids for the rest of their lives. Is that the kind of
country we want?"

Dr. Ellen L. Bassuk, a psychiatrist who is president of the
Better Homes Foundation, reports that homeless mothers who
are alcoholic or on crack are showing up in large numbers. Fetal
Alcohol Syndrome, she says, has replaced Down syndrome and
spina bifida as the leading cause of infant mental retardation.
"Substance abuse and family violence—not unrelated patholo-
gies—are the main cause of family homelessness throughout the
country," she said.

Compared to the problem of homeless families, housing for
the single homeless seems almost attainable. Mayor David N.
Dinkins is under pressure to build more than 10,000 S.R.O.
[single-room occupancy] units, a quick, relatively cheap fix. But
the rush to the S.R.O. bandwagon has already produced an an-
guished backlash from not-for-profit groups who operate more
than 2,000 S.R.O. units in Manhattan. A statement drafted by
Stephan Russo of the Goddard-Riverside Community Center
warned that by referring homeless men and women from emergency shelters without proper screening for drugs, alcohol, prior
hospitalization or criminal activity, the city was threatening the
stability and security of long-established neighborhood agencies.
"The notion of limited supportive housing sounds nice in principle," the statement declared, "but the reality is that the level of
need of those we are housing is far greater than our capacity to
respond. As a result, the 'new' nonprofit S.R.O.'s are in danger of
becoming nothing more than more humane repositories for the
shelter population fraught with the same problems of violence,
drug abuse and decompensation found in city shelters."

A case in point is the Senate, a completely renovated eight-
story, 136-room former shooting gallery and hangout for pimps
and prostitutes on West 92d Street, east of Broadway. Janice
Johns, the director of Social Services, says the police are called
three or four times a week to prevent violence, deter suicide, or
arrest a drug dealer. The building's own security force reports
two or three incidents a night: "Lorraine was arguing again with
her imaginary enemies." "Jorge is drunk and playing the radio
with incredible noise." "Luis pulled out a knife." Johns had not
expected this sort of trouble. "We didn't know about MICA"—the

acronym stands for Mentally Ill/Chemical Abuser—"and the city didn't tell us," she explained despairingly. But MICA's are in the minority; for most tenants, the Senate is the first quiet haven they have known in years.

Perhaps the most remarkable resident is the Senate's tenant association treasurer, a 44-year-old woman named Jay. She was in the Willowbrook mental hospital for 12 years, homeless for six years on the streets of the Bronx, and was raped, robbed and beaten before finding safety at the Traveler's Hotel for women near the Port Authority Bus Terminal, run by the West Side Cluster, among the larger of the city's hundreds of volunteer agencies for the homeless. Jay works as a volunteer at St. Luke's Hospital one day a week. One of her proudest possessions is a Mickey Mouse phone, which stands on a table in her spotless room. "I never had a private phone until I came to this beautiful home," she said. "And I'm not homeless anymore. What more can I ask."

The collective experience of Robert Hayes, Ellen Baxter and Kim Hopper, who met while working with the homeless more than a decade ago, shows how much ingenuity and persistence are required to get anything done. Hayes, fresh out of New York University Law School, got his first job with the blue-chip firm of Sullivan & Cromwell, and won a landmark pro bono case in 1981. Citing the State Constitution, he obtained a court order compelling City Hall to provide shelter for Robert Callahan, a homeless man; the municipal shelter program, now consisting of 10,000 beds, followed. Hayes, chairman of the Coalition for the Homeless, has begun another major legal assault, arguing in State Supreme Court that the city and state must create supportive housing for the mentally ill.

Ellen Baxter had been working at the Community Service Society since the summer of 1979, when she was a graduate student at the Columbia University School of Public Health. Hayes was putting together the Callahan case and Baxter helped him gather evidence. Later, she worked with Franciscan nuns who had opened a shelter for homeless people who were being removed from the Madison Square Garden area during the 1980 Democratic National Convention. "That's when the homeless coalition got off the ground," she said. In 1986, she opened the Heights, on West 178th Street, the first of four permanent S.R.O. buildings for the homeless. It took her three years of hacking through red tape to get the building gutted, rebuilt, financed, and finally filled with 55 single men and women who had been sleeping on the street.

Kim Hopper went to Columbia with Baxter and in 1981 was the co-author with her of "Private Lives/Public Spaces," a pioneering study that investigated the nature and origins of today's homelessness and is often cited in later, more academic, works. Hopper has a doctorate in medical anthropology. He organized the local effort by the United States Census Bureau to monitor its own count of the homeless by employing 127 observers, disguised as homeless people, who watched the official enumerators at work. Is there hope for homelessness? "I have mixed feelings," Hopper said. "Positively, there are hundreds of private shelters in the city, and people are more involved. On the other hand, the public is responding to society's traditional view of homelessness as a problem of damaged and disagreeable people."

Peter P. Smith heads the country's largest network of private aid to the homeless—almost 400 New York City churches and synagogues that supply emergency food, shelter and permanent housing through the Partnership for the Homeless. In March, the partnership opened a supportive residence for homeless people with AIDS, a group expected to number 100,000 nationally by 1995. "In the last 10 years we've learned what works and what doesn't work," Smith said. "Now, at least, the building blocks are in place."

Social scientists have pointed out that the Government virtually eliminated poverty among the elderly by enormous spending on Social Security (which helps explain, incidentally, why the median age of the homeless population has dropped to somewhere between 30 and 35). "For the first time in our history," writes the sociologist Peter H. Rossi, author of "Down and Out in America," "the poverty rate for persons aged 65 and over is less than that for the rest of the population." Now is the time, Rossi and others are suggesting, to raise the basic level of welfare benefits and even add a new category, Aid to Families With Dependent Adults, for those doubled-up families who are warding off homelessness by taking in relatives.

President Bush's own plans for helping the homeless rest largely on a $728 million housing proposal that advocates have welcomed more for its recognition of homelessness than as a seriously financed attack on it. About $450 million of the $728 million is restricted to vouchers that pay a monthly subsidy based

on the difference between a "fair market" rent and one-third of
the tenant's income. But, because the rent may exceed a "fair
market" level in tight markets that exist in many major cities
where the homeless need housing the most, vouchers are likely to
induce a landlord to raise his asking price.

One skeptic is James W. Rouse, a highly successful commercial
builder and developer, now retired, whose Enterprise Foundation
has provided expertise and funds since 1981 to 100 groups in 27
communities to develop affordable housing for the poor. "Vouchers do nothing to repair bombed-out neighborhoods and abandoned buildings," Rouse said. "It's outrageous to think you can
solve homelessness that way." According to Rouse, if the Federal
Government gave the states $3 billion coupled with matching
requirements, "it would have a tremendous impact at reasonable
cost. A thousand points of light sounds fine," he added, "but
there's no electricity."

Margery A. Turner, a housing specialist at the Urban Institute
in Washington, agreed that without more cheap housing there
could be "no solution and no prevention" of homelessness. And
that can't happen without a heavy Federal commitment, she
stressed. She didn't think that local housing solutions, no matter
how ingeniously financed or enthusiastically pursued, can be the
answer. "Even if there were a hundred Jim Rouses," she said,
"that's still not a national housing policy."

Housing in the United States is regarded as a commodity, not
a necessity. Production for profit is the game, but losers can't play.
And it will take more than billions of dollars spent on housing to
make a big difference in homelessness, which is only the most
extreme form of poverty. "We spend less on social welfare as a
percent of G.N.P. than any advanced industrialized country," said
Lee Bawden, a senior economist at the Urban Institute. "That's
the American way, but it's catching up with us on the homeless
issue." Deeply ingrained in American attitudes is the distinction
between the "deserving" and the "undeserving" poor. As the sociologist Daniel Bell put it in "The Cultural Contradictions of
Capitalism": "The United States, so strongly individualist in tem-
per, and so bourgeois in appetite, has never wholly mastered the
art of collective solutions, or of readily accepting the idea of a
public interest, as against private gain."

Bell's analysis helps explain why private philanthropy developed its unique social-welfare niche in America, and why President Bush was just echoing tradition when he called on armies of

volunteers to cope with homelessness. Despite an impressive response by thousands of local nonprofit groups, private exertions are clearly not the same thing as public policy, given the scale and complexity of homelessness. Moreover, unlike the elderly, the homeless have no constituency of children or Congressmen to give them voice; they don't even vote. Nor do the competing needs of education, health, drug control, deficit reduction or a crumbling infrastructure suggest that America's poor are about to cash in on any peace dividend. At H.U.D., for example, Anna Kondratas draws the line when asked whether higher Federal welfare payments for poor tenants might help stem homelessness: "We can't have socialism for the poor and capitalism for the wealthy."

Peter Rossi has estimated that in 1980 there were about 17 million "extremely poor" people in America; for a family of four, this meant an annual income of $4,396 or less—about half the Federal poverty line. Calculating further, he figures that with a rent bill of $200 a month, such a family would have been left with a daily budget of $1.50 to cover all other expenses. "Given the increased size since 1980 of the extremely poor population," Rossi concludes, "it is remarkable not that we have so many homeless people in America, but that we have so *few.*"

HOMELESSNESS IN AMERICA[3]

In recent years, greater media attention to the problem of homelessness in America has helped to bring to the attention of the public the magnitude of the homelessness problem and to break some of the traditional stereotypes of homeless persons. . . .

Even more startling than the sheer magnitude of the homeless problem itself are the demographics of the homeless population. With the move toward de-institutionalization in the past three decades, the percentage of the homeless mentally ill has

[3]Article by Charles E. King, former Sturgis Fellow at Corpus Christi College of the University of Cambridge in Cambridge, England, from *The Humanist* 49:8+ My/Je '89. Copyright © 1989 by The American Humanist Association. Reprinted by permission.

risen sharply. In 1955, the population of public psychiatric hospitals was 559,000, but by 1981 that figure had dropped to around 122,000, accounting for the American Psychiatric Association's estimate that 20 to 50 percent of homeless persons are seriously mentally ill.

Children, too, account for a growing percentage of the homeless. If one may extrapolate from figures in a Pennsylvania study by Temple University, as much as 15 percent of the homeless population may be children under five years of age. And in a recent Harvard University study of 151 children living with their families in shelters, nearly half of them of preschool age showed at least one developmental lag on the Denver Developmental Screening Test, and one-third had two or more lags. According to Ellen Bassuk, a homelessness researcher, "Many were depressed and anxious and had severe learning difficulties; 43 percent had repeated a grade, and about one-fourth were in special classes."

Perhaps surprisingly, a Baltimore study conducted by the National Institute of Mental Health showed that one-half to two-thirds of the homeless persons surveyed had completed high school, and 25 to 30 percent had completed college. Similarly, 22 percent of the homeless persons polled in a recent U.S. Conference of Mayors survey had full- or part-time jobs. Although studies disagree on exact figures, it is clear that the stereotype of the "bum," the uneducated free-loader who chooses to be homeless—if it ever were an accurate portrayal—certainly no longer fits.

In a political system in which policy decisions are made according to strictly utilitarian criteria, questions of the magnitude of the homeless problem and the profile of the shelter population are important. Even though the efforts of the media must be lauded for helping to make homelessness a political issue, concentrating on numbers and percentages in recent reportage has necessarily obscured what may well be some of the central questions of the homeless problem: what, in more human terms, does it mean to be homeless, and why ought we help the homeless in the first place?

It is of more than semantic significance, I think, that we call these people "homeless" instead of "houseless" or "shelterless." In our culture, the idea of a home connotes more than just a physical shelter. A *home* offers a sense of security, of permanence, of one's own *space*. In fact, where we live, where we are *from*, is often the quintessential source of our self-identity. Perhaps the defining characteristic of homelessness, which often seems to be ignored, is the homeless person's total lack of support—physical, financial, emotional, spiritual. As writer David Whitman has said, the homeless are decidedly different from other poor persons in at least one significant respect: "They are profoundly alone."

That at least *something* should be done to aid the homeless no longer seems to be a serious point for debate. Liberals and conservatives alike advocate, in greater or lesser degrees, job training programs, housing projects, and other forms of aid and only the most uninformed persons still speak of the entire homeless population as "bums." But even to persons actively involved in seeking solutions to the homeless problem, nagging questions often arise: why ought we help the homeless in the first place, and how can we convince others that they ought to be concerned? Responses to these questions vary. Churches seem to donate to shelter programs perhaps in part as an exercise in Christian charity, and attempt—as Jesus did—to see God in the hungry, the thirsty, and the naked. Secular groups, though, often rely upon appeals to basic human compassion or, in some cases, to enlightened self-interest—approaches that have little moral impact on the compassionless or the unenlightened.

But these approaches aside, perhaps the question of eliminating homelessness in America ultimately comes down to fulfilling our part of a bargain—to undertaking a kind of social contract. Inasmuch as we benefit from our choice to live in a society that encourages economic competition and rewards personal initiative, it is incumbent on us to help those who have somehow been left behind in the race for economic success. And considering the alienation of the poor from the sources of political and economic power—their inability to represent themselves in the political forums that we have created—a fundamental maxim becomes clear: if we accept the benefits of the system, we must necessarily accept the responsibilities. . . .

Since homelessness is not a monolithic problem, any comprehensive solution must address substance abuse, mental illness, disease, and the plethora of other social ills that have become results—if not causes—of homelessness. But it is clear that the solution must begin with our going beyond the numbers and percentages, understanding what being homeless means in human terms, and agreeing that "securing the blessings of liberty" is as much the job of individuals as it is the task of the federal government. We must affirm, with Peter Marin of *Harper's,* that responding to the problem of homelessness in America does not translate into the language of "conservatives" or "liberals." Homelessness, in its most fundamental terms, is "the *sum total* of our dreams, policies, intentions, errors, omissions, cruelties, kindnesses, all of it recorded in flesh, in the life of the street."

II. THE FACES OF HOMELESSNESS

EDITOR'S INTRODUCTION

The articles in this section attempt to put a face on the homeless beyond statistics and their coded implications. Most of the authors have done what most of us have not: they have actually talked with the homeless. As a result, two things become strikingly clear—the humanity of these displaced people and the realization that anywhere in the United States one is never very far from someone who is homeless.

Writing in *The New Republic* Professor John J. DiIulio, Jr. examines a number of academic studies and theories of the past decade on the subject of homelessness in America. In addition, he provides significant insight into public policies which have added to the problem, with particular emphasis placed on the developments of the 1980s and the Reagan administration.

The second article, written for *The Washington Monthly* by Scott Shuger, takes a more subjective approach, in which the main focus is a journey through Washington, DC's homeless population by the author, posing as a homeless man himself at times. Through conversations and observations, the author introduces us to the panoply of the urban homeless in Washington. He concludes that besides mental health problems and substance abuse as causes of homelessness there exists an abstract quality displayed by many of the people he meets in the course of his journey—he calls it the X-factor. Implicit in this phenomenon is the conviction that many of the homeless will remain so because they choose to, having given up on society. Interesting to this analysis is the author's belief that failure to recognize and address the X-factor may be at the heart of why neither liberals nor conservatives can get a handle on effective strategies for confronting homelessness.

Two articles follow that explore homelessness in two places where most would be surprised to find it—in one of the country's wealthiest suburbs and in the heartland of rural America. In *The Nation* freelance writer Brad Kessler travels to Westchester County in New York to discover the homeless living in the shadows of the Rockefeller estate and not far from the corporate mecca known as the "Platinum Mile." An article from *USA Today* reveals a threefold rise in rural homelessness in less than a decade. The causes for the homeless in both places are the same, namely, a lack of affordable housing made worse by few, if any, alternatives such as shelters. The homeless in these two communities are also similar, with a larger number of families with children among the victims.

Finally, *Phi Delta Kappan* reports on the population that has experienced the most alarming growth in homelessness—children. Authors Sally Reed and R. Craig Sautter paint a bleak picture for our nation's youth. Among other horrifying statistics, the authors quote U.S. Department of Education estimates that almost one quarter of a million children are homeless, with the number increasing. Among the factors to blame for the problem, the authors cite the economy of the last decade with its tendency to favor the wealthy at the expense of the indigent; a poor or nonexistant health care system; and the ineffectiveness of legislative solutions.

THERE BUT FOR FORTUNE[1]

From 1972 to 1980, "Downtown" Willie Brown was my close friend. During that time, which for me stretched the life-defining distance from eighth grade to my first year of graduate study, I was one all-purpose set of hands in my father's pizzeria in center city Philadelphia and Willie was the other. For nine years we spent most weekends together, working, talking, and joking, though mostly (as my father frequently and loudly testified) talking and joking.

A black man born and raised in Portsmouth, Virginia, Willie migrated alone to Philly sometime in the late 1950s. He chose Philadelphia because he'd heard that the city had "lots of good jobs for colored folk." But for years all he could find was unstable "dollar-a-day" labor as a barroom porter. "Nights came," he re-

[1]Article by John J. DiIulio Jr., from *The New Republic* 204:27+ Je 24 '91. Copyright © 1991 by The New Republic, Inc. Reprinted with permission.

counted, "when wasn't nothing between me and skid row but three blocks." When the pizzeria opened, he wandered in and asked for a full-time job "doing whatever needs doing." Lots of other obviously down and out men had wandered in and made the same request, but for some reason my father hired him on the spot, and he soon became an indispensable worker and a friend of the family.

But Willie was surprised and disappointed by what he found in the City of Brotherly Love, a disappointment he often expressed by saying, "Jesus Christ, there ain't no difference from here to there, no difference at all. Y'all have as many bad words for poor and colored folk here as south, maybe more!" On his journey north, he smoked pot, drank too much, and was, as he put it, "taken for crazy by a lot of folk, which a little bit I was and surely am." He also took a detour or two to prison, where he "split some head" to keep from being raped or robbed, and gladly did extra time behind bars for the privilege.

Willie was illiterate, and he knew what that cost him. "Things in this here life be a horse of a different color," he used to say, "if I could make out my letters." I made many attempts to teach him how to read, but they were all in vain. Within an hour of every session, he always managed to transform our tutoring table into an arm-wrestling platform: "A's for 'arm-wrestling,' son, so let's you and me get to it!"

Although he did his best to hide it from me for fear that I might be ashamed of him (and, no doubt, for fear that I might take his frequent anti-drug sermons less seriously), I knew that he never gave up his "reefer," as he called it, and that he sold a little on the street, and did some small-time pimping, to "get me some nice things before I'm dead enough not to have 'em." On more than one occasion, I covered for him on the job when he was too drunk to work, carted him to the flea-bag hotel room he called home, and put him to bed.

Nobody, including Willie, knew precisely how old he was, but when we celebrated his birthday on April 1, 1980, we called it his 50th. Shortly after that, the pizzeria went under. By then I lived in Cambridge, and within a few years I completely lost track of Willie—until a subfreezing December night in 1988, when I drove through center city Philadelphia after a frenzied bout of Christmas shopping. I saw a man on a streetcorner opposite my car. He was aggressively panhandling; he wasn't wearing a coat; he was shouting what through the distance magnified by my tightly rolled car windows sounded like obscenities; he looked frail and filthy. And he looked vaguely like Willie. I quickly decided that this "homeless person" wasn't him. I made my turn, sped on, and forgot about it.

Reading some of the recent literature on the homeless in America brought that episode back to me, not painlessly. It also persuaded me that, despite the many remaining gaps in our knowledge about the nature, the extent, and the causes of homelessness in the world's most affluent society, and despite the political, legal, administrative, and budgetary impossibility of solving the problem through any single national public policy, there is much that can be done—by individuals, by private organizations, and by governments—to help the homeless, to improve the prospects of the near-homeless, and to prevent as-yet-unborn citizens from becoming homeless. The conventional wisdom about the sources and the scope of homelessness in America is misleading. The mounting hopelessness about solutions is ungrounded.

According to the 1990 report of the U.S. Conference of Mayors, over the last year or so public sentiment toward the homeless has hardened in over half of the nation's cities. But take even a short walk in the shoes of the homeless—men and women, black, white, and brown, young and old, drunk and sober, mentally healthy and mentally ill, families and loners, poor, poorer, and poorest—as James Wright invites us to do in *Address Unknown*, and you will see just how inadequate the new hard-heartedness is. Civic toughness, whether in the form of bootcamp prisons, tightly run shelters, no-nonsense drug therapies, or work-based welfare programs, has its limits, especially when the social problems at which it's aimed have deep economic roots.

For a start, we must acknowledge two things. First, nobody knows precisely how many homeless people there are in America. Second, this ignorance does not present a major barrier to fashioning effective responses to the situation. Clearly the scale of the problem is relevant, and homelessness is a national poverty problem. But the needs of homeless Americans—for social services and other support—vary greatly, and the economic and other influences that foster homelessness differ from place to place. Innovative national policies might help, but an all-encompassing, "top-down" response to this complex problem is less likely to succeed than an incremental, multilevel approach.

Estimates of the number of homeless in America vary wildly, and disputes over the meaning and measurement of homelessness abound. In *Down and Out in America,* a state-of-the-numbers-game study, Peter Rossi, a professor of sociology at the University of Massachusetts—Amherst, makes a simple but important distinction between the "literal homeless" and the "precariously housed." The literal homeless are those who don't have "customary and regular access to a conventional dwelling" (houses, apartments, mobile homes, rented rooms). They live and sleep in places that were not intended for living and sleeping, "including public areas such as bus stations or lobbies, abandoned buildings, dormitory arrangements (as in shelters), cars, vans, trucks, and scrap-metal shacks." The precariously housed are poor people who are about to be evicted, about to be thrown out of the house by relatives, can't meet the raised rent, and so on.

Many advocates for the homeless maintain that between 1.5 and 3 million Americans are, on any given night, literally homeless. This range has been enshrined by print and broadcast journalists, but it is almost certainly a gross overestimate. Every credible study puts the number of literally homeless in America at half a million or under. A study by the Department of Housing and Urban Development in 1984 estimated the number of literally homeless to be between 250,000 and 300,000. The HUD report did not deny the methodological difficulties involved in arriving at reliable estimates, and even allowed for a more elastic range of between 192,000 and 586,000.

Still, advocates for the homeless howled that the HUD study was nothing but a pseudoscientific propaganda weapon in the Reagan administration's "war against the poor." Two years later, however, a report prepared for the National Bureau of Economic Research (NBER) by Richard Freeman and Brian Hall, two independent and highly respected Harvard scholars, reanalyzed the HUD data and estimated that in 1986, 350,000 Americans were literally homeless. In 1988 a careful study by the Urban Institute put the number between 567,000 and 600,000, noting that, if anything, the estimate erred on the high side. The federal government has based its working numbers on the Urban Institute's estimates. Given "available information and reasonable assumptions," Rossi concludes, "the most believable national estimate is that at least 300,000 people are homeless each night in this country, and possibly as many as 400,000 to 500,000 if one accepts growth rates in the past few years of between 10 percent and 20 percent." He estimates that another 4 to 7 million Americans are so poor as to be precariously housed.

Presumably, advocates for the homeless are interested in confronting the problem, not in prolonging tedious, quasi-academic, and often politicized debates about the numbers, the main effect of which is to delay action. The real questions that need addressing are not quantitative. They have to do with the identity of these unfortunates, and with the reasons for their condition. Who are the homeless? Why are they homeless? What, if anything, can be done about their plight?

According to the profile of the urban homeless assembled in the 1990 report of the U.S. Conference of Mayors, 51 percent are single men, 34 percent are families with children, 12 percent are single women, and 3 percent are "unaccompanied youth." The racial composition of this extremely impoverished population is predictably skewed: 46 percent black, 34 percent white, 15 percent Hispanic. And, not surprising, the incidence of life-destroying problems among the homeless is far higher than in the general population: 38 percent are substance abusers, 28 percent are mentally ill, 76 percent have been chronically unemployed.

The reigning view is that homelessness is primarily a poverty problem. Rossi, Wright, and several other leading analysts argue that a straightforward housing supply and demand disparity accounts for most of the people on the street. The crux of the problem, Wright maintains, has been "too many poor chasing too few affordable housing units." He offers lots of statistical evidence to support his case, typified by the following Philadelphia story:

Between 1978 and 1982, the number of low-income rental units in that city fell by 26 percent, from about 211,000 units to 157,000. During that same period, the size of Philadelphia's poverty population rose from 516,000 to 708,000, an increase of 37 percent. Simple division shows that in the late 1970s, there were 2.4 poor people in Philadelphia for each available low-income unit. Four years later, there were 4.5 poor people per available unit. The housing squeeze faced by Philadelphia's poor is unmistakable. That there is nowhere else to go (but the streets) is not an excuse. It has become an inescapable fact of the political economy of Philadelphia and many other cities.

But as purely quantitative analyses of social problems usually are, this portrait of the problem is much too simple. Serious critics of this view have raised at least three important questions, the answers to which reveal a considerably more complicated situation. First, if homelessness in America is fundamentally a poverty problem, then how come the problem worsened in the 1970s and early 1980s, when the fraction of American citizens living in poverty shrank from its 1960s level? Second, is the problem a lack of

affordable housing caused by Reagan-era cutbacks in public assistance, as the most polemical versions of the position have it? Or
have local government policies had the perverse if unintended
effect of restricting the stock of low-income units, inducing some
of the extremely poor to become homeless? And third, how can
homelessness be viewed mainly as a poverty problem when so
many of the homeless are physically debilitated, mentally ill,
or both?

Some advocates for the homeless simply deny that there are
proportionately fewer poor Americans today than there were in
1965, when the War on Poverty was launched. By every credible
measure, in the early 1980s, the fraction of Americans living in
poverty increased. But the fact is that the poverty population has
shrunk over the last quarter century. (The Census Bureau over-
states the total number of poor because it undercounts the incomes and assets of low-income households.) That's not to say that
the story has been one of unmitigated improvement. As many
crossed the poverty line, those Americans who remained extremely poor became more concentrated than ever before in the
nation's economically depressed inner cities. In a series of reports
for the National League of Cities, Mark Hughes, a professor of
public affairs at Princeton, has documented this trend and aptly
characterized the nation's post-War-on-Poverty inner cities as
pockets of "isolated deprivation." Many of those who became
homeless in the 1970s and early 1980s, perhaps most of them,
were recruited from these dispossessed metropolitan heartlands
on the economic fringe of urban communities that were themselves on the economic fringe.

Today's homeless Americans, according to Henry Miller, a
professor of social welfare at Berkeley, are the direct socioeconomic descendants of the men, women, and children who
throughout history have fallen "outside the pale of convention by
virtue of a feeble attachment to hearth and home"—beggars and
vagrants, Forty-Niners and hoboes, Hoovervillites and Joads. Like
Rossi and Wright, Miller, in *On the Fringe,* juggles relevant numbers to argue that homelessness is essentially a poverty problem,
concluding dryly that "people of means, with rare and trivial
exceptions, do not become homeless." But he usefully complicates
the voguish distinction between the "old homeless" and the "new
homeless" that underlies most of the purely economic arguments
about the causes and cures of homelessness.

This distinction is based on a demographically demonstrable

shift. Today's homeless are mainly minority adults in their early to mid-30s with some formal education beyond grade school. Yesterday's homeless consisted mainly of uneducated older white men living on skid row. Among today's homeless are large numbers of female-headed families without any substance abuse problems. The vast majority of yesterday's homeless were broken-down alcoholic men. The new homeless are virtually shut out of a high-tech economy in which menial jobs requiring little mental or physical dexterity are scarce and do not pay a living wage. Within walking distance of most skid row flophouses, the old homeless had their labor market niche in low-but-livable-wage work such as muscling truck cargo or day-labor construction jobs. In the 1960s and 1970s, however, the mechanization of such work (forklifts, containerized shipping), and the unionization of the construction and stevedore industries, obliterated this casual labor market in urban areas.

As Rossi observes, these developments put both the old homeless and skid row "out of business." Or, as Wright explains, "The historical means to avoid literal homelessness have been largely removed from the urban scene. . . . The income function of casual labor has been replaced by scavenging from trash cans and by panhandling. The organized social system of skid row, in short, has been replaced by the disorganized existence of homelessness."

Miller accepts that today's homeless differ demographically from yesterday's, and he recognizes that recent changes in the labor market have given rise to "a new generation of vagrant and homeless." But viewing homeless Americans of the 1980s in the broad sweep of Western history, he concludes that the "homeless of today are not very much different from those of yesteryear." Economically the "new homeless" are fundamentally what the homeless have always been: namely, "on the extreme edge of the labor force." Behaviorally Miller finds as many similarities as differences between the inhabitants of skid row and the dispossessed ghetto youth, both male and female, who came after them.

Most timely of all is Miller's recitation of the underlying similarities between how society-at-large responds to the homeless of today and how it responded to the wandering poor of earlier eras. Then as now, the basic attitude "has been harsh, unsympathetic, and—all too often—downright draconian in its severity." Yesterday's homeless person was

whipped, branded, jailed, transported, indentured, enslaved, or executed; in less harsh times, he was scorned, shunned, harassed, or pushed

out of the community. Today, the vilification of the homeless is couched in
a language of surface neutrality: he or she is "mentally ill," "alcoholic,"
"drug-addicted," "pauperized."

But actions speak more truly than words, and, as Miller suggests,
while overall poverty levels in the United States have declined,
our society has been content to let its inner-city streets become
one more chapter in the story of the other America.

But that story is not quite the black and white tale that is
commonly told. The chief villain is typically Ronald Reagan, during whose administration certain kinds of federal assistance for
low-income housing declined dramatically. The basic plot is as
follows. Between 1980 and 1988, the Reagan administration cut
budget authority for all federal housing assistance programs by
82 percent, from $32 billion to $5.7 billion, and gutted Section 8
of the Housing and Community Development Act of 1974. Section 8 provided low-income renters with housing certificates that
guaranteed landlords the difference between a tenant's rent and
30 percent of his income. It was not established as an entitlement
program; certificates were issued on an "as available" basis involving cumbersome applications procedures. Thus it was easy for the
administration to slash the number of new certificates issued
from 110,000 in 1981 to 10,000 in 1988.

At the same time, the Reagan administration did nothing to
expand the stock of public housing. From 1977 to 1981 the
federal government authorized some 215,000 new public housing
units, but only 44,000 were authorized from 1982 to 1988. As a
direct result of these Reagan cutbacks, in the 1980s thousands of
low-income people who in the 1970s would have been kept from
the streets by federal assistance joined the ranks of the homeless.

That much is true, but it's only half of the story. A closer look
at the record reveals that the Reagan administration refocused,
rather than razed, the federal government's housing assistance
policies, and did so as part of a broader effort to recast federal
anti-poverty measures in accordance with (like them or not) conservative principles.

For starters, we need to remind ourselves that a federal dollar
authorized for tomorrow is not a federal dollar spent today. The
Reagan administration did cut *authorized* spending (that is, com-
mitments to spend money at some future date) for federal housing assistance by 82 percent, but between 1980 and 1988 total
outlays on housing subsidies of low-income households actually
more than doubled, from $5.7 billion to $13.8 billion, and the

total number of low-income households receiving federal housing
subsidies increased from an estimated 3.3 million to 4.4 million.

A similar but slightly more complicated reality lies behind the
saga of Section 8 certificates. The Ford and Carter administrations
were committed to expanding the nation's public housing
stock, and they used the Section 8 program to do it. As William
Tucker has documented in *The Excluded Americans*, during those
years developers who agreed to construct new low-income housing
units received blocs of Section 8 certificates sufficient to fill
their entire buildings. (The rest of the certificates were set aside
for tenants in existing housing, and for the "substantial and moderate
rehabilitation" of existing housing.)

Section 8 certificates thus put money directly in the pockets of
developers rather than in the pockets of the poor. Although Section
8 awards had always gone to developers with good political
connections, during the Reagan years the program became a political
cesspool in which well-connected Republicans received
huge consulting fees to influence the high-ranking HUD officials
responsible for awarding the certificates.

The Reagan administration, however, had never endorsed the
basic idea behind the Section 8 program, namely that the nation's
supply of low-income housing needed to be expanded. In 1982,
in *The Report of the President's Commission on Housing*, the administration
declared that, rather than go on building public housing,
federal housing policy should put more income directly in the
hands of the needy. In keeping with that declaration, it introduced
a housing voucher program in 1984. The vouchers were
established as five-year rent supplements handed directly to low-income
tenants. Vouchers cost $4,500 a year, as opposed to
$9,000 a year for a new unit of public housing. Between 1984 and
1988, although the administration issued only 121,000 new Section
8 certificates (fewer than were issued by the Carter administration
in 1979 alone), it issued 202,000 housing vouchers.

Finally, although the Reagan administration did reverse plans
for future federal public housing construction, new units of public
housing increased faster in the Reagan years than they did in
the 1970s. From 1977 to 1980, for example, about 41,000 new
units became available, an average of 10,250 units each year. But
from 1981 to 1988, some 165,000 new units came on line, an
average of 20,625 a year.

Of course, the Reagan administration deserves no credit for
the expansion in new public housing units that occurred on its

watch. (There are still some public housing units in the pipeline from the Ford administration.) And no one can accuse Reagan of making HUD, under the stewardship of the model anti-public servant Samuel Pierce, into a bastion of progressive thought and pragmatic action aimed at America's poverty problems. Still, despite the large cutbacks in authorizations, the Reagan years were, in Tucker's words, "actually boom years for public housing," a fact that strongly undercuts the view that a slackened federal effort in public housing is the main cause of homelessness. As current HUD deputy Anna Kondratas writes in a[n] issue of *American Psychologist,* "Housing assistance spending actually rose every year during the 1980s," and more affordable housing has been lost to "urban renewal, inflation-driven speculation, tax policy, and other such phenomena than to any putative federal budget cuts."

In any case, merely pointing to failures in federal public housing policy doesn't begin to account for the full dimensions of the problem, as Thomas Main showed three years ago. (Main, I must note, is a doctoral candidate writing his dissertation at Princeton under my supervision.) He reported that between 1979 and 1983 the number of public housing units in New York City actually increased by 72,000 to 1.25 million, but not enough to keep pace with the increase in the number of extremely poor inner-city residents looking for such units. He argued that the gap could have been closed by dividing up old public housing units, renovating abandoned buildings, and creating other accommodations of inferior quality that would have been better than a one-way ticket to the streets.

But this demand for low-income housing was never met, he concluded, "because housing regulations in New York (and some other cities) made it difficult for the market to adjust." So difficult, in fact, that when the city offered landlords a "bonus" of $9,700 to put up homeless families, there were few takers, since "participating landlords would have had to spend more than the bonus to bring their buildings up to the required standard." The pivotal role of local housing regulations, as opposed to federal government cutbacks, in fostering homelessness also emerges in a recent study by Tucker that argues that, other things being equal, housing regulations are a major cause of homelessness. Housing shortages, including shortages of low-income housing, are largely "a local problem created by local regulation, which is the work of municipal governments."

Still more evidence that homelessness is not merely a function of a federally induced lack of affordable housing comes from those who argue that local government policies themselves have, in the words of economist Randall Filer, "caused much of the problem by creating powerful incentives for poor families to become homeless." In an article in the new magazine *NY*, Filer reveals that though the rate of homelessness among single people in New York City is only about one-third that in other major cities, the rate of homelessness among families (mainly single women and their children) in the city is nearly twice as high. In essence, he argues convincingly that, relative to other cities, New York's housing and social welfare policies make homelessness pay for poor families, but not for poor singles.

In contrast to homeless families in other jurisdictions, for example, New York's homeless families are more likely than not to receive food stamps, welfare payments, and other government support. And compared with poor families in New York who remain precariously housed with relatives or have pieced together other private arrangements, poor families who declare themselves to be homeless and enter the city's shelter system immediately gain priority access to subsidized housing and increased disposable cash income.

And the perverse incentives do not end there. Once inside the system, pregnant women (and new mothers) receive priority over other homeless women for permanent placement in subsidized housing, and they are guaranteed temporary placement in a private room or hotel. Thus, notes Filer, there is "an active street market in pregnant women's urine, bought by non-pregnant women who wish to secure" these benefits, and "the city's policies may also encourage some women to bear children they cannot support."

During the 1980s advocates for the homeless and most analysts rejected such "supply-creates-demand" arguments as so much conservative claptrap. They can no more. Indeed, last October that very thesis was argued by David Dinkins, who was quoted in *The New York Times* explaining a spike in the demand for spots in his city's welfare hotels this way: "Unintentionally, an incentive for people to use welfare hotels has been created. Families are frequently entering our city shelter system in order to find an apartment. We do not want doubled-up families to make themselves homeless in order to find an apartment."

It is misleading, therefore, to diagnose homelessness in America as merely a straightforward problem of "too many poor chasing too few affordable housing units." Much the same can be said of the conventional view that homelessness in America has grown largely as a result of the deinstitutionalization of the mentally ill. The effects of deinstitutionalization in fostering homelessness have been greatly exaggerated. In 1955 the population of state hospitals for the mentally ill peaked at 559,000; today it stands at about 100,000. In *Out of Bedlam,* Ann Braden Johnson, a director of mental health services for women in New York City's jail system, explains that efforts to depopulate state mental hospitals began in the 1940s, not, as is commonly believed, in the 1960s. The alluring premise of deinstitutionalization was that treating the mentally ill in small, community-based mental health centers, instead of large, bureaucratic state mental institutions, would improve treatment, preserve dignity, and save money.

In the 1960s and early 1970s three developments spurred the deinstitutionalization movement. First, the pharmaceutical industry aggressively marketed the "wonder drug" Thorazine and other psychotropic medications that, as Johnson puts it, made mental patients "easier to handle," and (or so it was predicted) better candidates for community-based treatment. Second, leaders of organized psychiatry articulated and enforced within their ranks a community mental health orthodoxy. In Johnson's unforgiving but not unpersuasive telling, the psychiatry profession "had turned its back on the chronic patients in the mental hospitals before."

Third, and of greatest continuing significance, federal judges, beginning with the Lessard decision in 1972, issued rulings that made it impossible to confine the mentally ill against their will unless they were found by a court of law to be immediately "dangerous" to themselves or others. The judges also mandated that any forced treatment of the mentally ill be administered in the least restrictive setting possible. On the platform provided by these decisions, ideologically driven civil liberties lawyers and financially-driven community mental health operators have lobbied effectively against any measures that might check deinstitutionalization.

It is not surprising that most of the patients discharged from mental institutions in the 1960s and early 1970s did not find adequate treatment in the community, because the blueprints for such treatment were never really drafted. No level of government did much to install the needed network of community mental health centers, or to realize in some other way the ideal of individualized treatment for the mentally ill. Failed by organized psychiatry and public administration, the deinstitutionalized were also failed by laboratory science as the curative properties of many psychotropic drugs proved to be little more than sales hype. Worst of all, however, they were failed by the communities that received them. As Oliver Sachs has observed, in "a large, bustling, indifferent city, such as New York," deinstitutionalization had no chance of success.

But how much did the folly of deinstitutionalization really contribute to the tragedy of homelessness? According to Rael Jean Isaac and Virginia C. Armat in *Madness in the Streets*, the conventional answer is the right one: lots, though they're not specific about how many of today's homeless are yesterday's deinstitutionalized. Reliable estimates don't exist, but it's certain that a more than negligible fraction of the discharged mental patients of the 1960s and early 1970s became homeless. Still, given that today's homeless are mainly young adults, and given that deinstitutionalization was implemented over a decade ago, the case against understanding homelessness in the 1980s as "madness in the streets" seems quite strong, as Johnson persuasively argues. By the mid-1970s, nearly everyone slated to be deinstitutionalized already had been. Isaac and Armat counter that we must take note of "the accumulation of helpless people released in successive waves as hospitals emptied," and count as victims of deinstitutionalization "the 'uninstitutionalized' population on the street—the chronically mentally ill young people who years ago would have gone to state mental hospitals."

Their book is excellent in many ways, not least of all in documenting the need to make involuntary commitment of the severely mentally ill easier. But without suspending logic and ignoring the best available statistics, it is impossible to find deinstitutionalization among the leading causes of contemporary homelessness. In the NBER study, for example, Freeman and Hall reported that only 1 percent of their sample had come to the streets or shelters directly from mental hospitals. And Wright reported that in a survey of 30,000 homeless people in sixteen cities, recent release from a mental institution "was judged the single most important reason for the homelessness of a mere 2 percent and a major factor for an additional 4 percent."

Still, if laws were changed to make involuntary institutionalization of the severely mentally ill easier, as Isaac and Armat strongly recommend, some fraction of today's mentally ill homeless population would no longer be exposed to the dangers of life on the streets. Unfortunately, no data exist to tell us what proportion of the current homeless population might be affected by such changes. It is worth noting, however, that in the survey reported by Wright, chronic mental illness was the chief reason for the homelessness of 16 percent of the respondents and a secondary factor for another 18 percent. . . .

[The final part of this article appears in Section Four of this compilation.]

WHO ARE THE HOMELESS?[2]

For anyone living in a city, the dilemma unfolds dozens of times a day: There he is, between me and my immediate goal— The Man With The Styrofoam Cup, asking me a simple question: "Spare some change?" That question lights off others of my own that go unspoken: "What does this guy do with the money?" "How much does he make a day?" "Doesn't begging like this make him feel awful?" "Why doesn't it make him feel awful enough to stop and get a job?" "How did he get in this fix?" "Is he really in a fix, or is he taking me for a sucker?" "Why should I give to this guy rather than the other beggars on the block?" "Or do they think I can give to them all?"

"Spare some change?" comes up because I am in a limited way accessible to The Man With The Styrofoam Cup. My questions come up because he is in a radical way inaccessible to me. To most of us, the homeless are a visible mystery. Perhaps some of the most hardened among us would prefer them to be invisible. But the rest of us would prefer them to be less of a mystery. We want to help, yes, but we want our efforts to go where they will make a difference. For that to happen, we have to know what we're up against.

[2]Article by Scott Shuger, an editor of *The Washington Monthly,* from *The Washington Monthly* 22:38+ Mr '90. Copyright © 1990 by the Washington Monthly Company, 1611 Connecticut Avenue, N.W., Washington, D.C. 20009. Reprinted with permission.

Hype for the Holidays

Although there have been some harder-edged stories on the homeless, the main message the media delivers about them is that despite their predicament, they're just like us. In a news special, Tom Brokaw stated that the homeless are "people you know." Robert Hayes, director of the National Coalition for the Homeless, told *The New York Times* that when he is contacted by television news programs or congressional committees looking at homelessness, "they always want white, middle-class people to interview." A recent study that examined the national print and broadcast coverage given the homeless between November 1986 and February 1989 discovered that a quarter of the homeless people featured in stories were children. That was equal to the number of those identified as unemployed and three times the number identified as substance abusers. Only 4 percent of the stories attributed the plight of the homeless to their personal problems.

A recent publication of the Better Business Bureau reported, "Many of those living in shelters or on the street are no different from those with a place to live. . . . Being on the street is often something out of their control." In a *New York Times* op-ed piece, Rep. Charles Schumer wrote that "the slightest misstep or misfortune—a temporary layoff, a large medical bill, a divorce—could send [a low-income] family onto the streets. Indeed that's exactly what's been happening." The concrete examples of the homeless Schumer cited are a working mother of eight whose eldest is an honor student, and a 63-year-old woman forced to retire from her job as a waitress because of arthritis. In another *Times* op-ed piece entitled "The Homeless: Victims of Prejudice," two Ivy League law students said that the homeless people they met during a summer of intern work included a Broadway playwright, a highly decorated World War II veteran, and an ex-professional basketball player. Not to mention "pregnant women who lost the race to stay one step ahead of the housing marshal, students trying to study in noisy shelters, and average families working diligently to save enough money for an apartment."

Jonathan Kozol, in his book on homeless families, *Rachel and Her Children,* features: a couple who, after their house burns down, lose their five children to foster homes and are reduced to panhandling; a 35-year-old woman, a college graduate who worked for many years before medical complications wiped out her savings, forced her to lose her home, ended her marriage, made her give up her kids, and left her sleeping on the beach; and a teacher, who when the heater in her building failed, was "in a matter of weeks . . . reduced from working woman and house-holder to a client of the welfare system." To the question "Why are they without homes?" Kozol responds, "Unreflective answers might retreat to explanations with which readers are familiar: 'family breakdown,' 'drugs,' 'culture of poverty,' 'teen pregnancies,' 'the underclass,' etc. While these are precipitating factors for some people, they are not the cause of homelessness. *The cause of homelessness is lack of housing.*" (Italics in the original.)

[In 1989] . . . the Salvation Army came out with a special TV commercial to boost its Christmas campaign for the homeless in New York City: *On the sidewalk in front of a wrought-iron fence, framed by a shopping bag on one side and a suitcase on the other, there's a mother and her child together in a sleeping bag, their white skins reflecting the street lights. As a man carrying a briefcase walks by, the child sits up; you can see her long blonde hair now. The mother kisses the girl and pulls her back down, hugging and patting her as they drift back to sleep.* "Home for the Holidays," the ad's caption says.

Honor students and playwrights, college graduates sleeping on the beach, mothers and daughters sleeping in the park—this is what I can read about or see on TV. But this is not what I see in Washington. Where in all this is the Man With The Styrofoam Cup?

Although real homeless people are all around me every day, I've been vulnerable to the more idealized representations of the press because my approach to street people has been typical of the white middle class: Usually, I stare straight ahead and walk on by, my head full of those skeptical questions. Sometimes, something—an excess of change, a particularly good day, or just a weariness of skepticism—would make me stop and give some money. But no matter what, there was one thing I would never, ever, do: Talk to these people. Recently, however, I decided to break that nervous middle class habit. I resolved to talk to the homeless, to ask them some of the questions I had been keeping to myself in all the years of walking right by.

Nights of Wine and Poses

I first put my new approach into effect one night last winter. On the stretch of Connecticut Avenue just above Dupont Circle, it was cold and rainy, and the panhandlers were huddled in bunches near the entrances of the restaurants on the block. With most of the dinner crowd already gone, the best pickings were over for the day. That left only pedestrians like me.

Two men come up to me, styrofoam cups in hand: "Spare some change?" Both men are unsteady on their feet and hard to understand, with 100-proof breath. I make a donation and learn that the tall black man is named Mike and the short one is K.C. I ask them how long they've been on the streets, and they tell me six months. They've both had jobs in construction. Mike says he used to work as a bartender until he lost his job because of his drinking. When I ask where they stay at night, Mike says that the owner of an art gallery across the street lets them sleep in the lobby of the building. Mike says they get to bathe every two days at a shelter in Alexandria.

"What do you do with the money you get?" I ask. Mike gives me a thumb-to-the-lip bottle motion. Then he shrugs his shoulders in embarrassment. "I got to go to a program. An in-patient program so I cain't get out so I cain't mess up. I got to clean my act up."

Mike is very polite, calling me "sir" frequently and saying "excuse me" to every passerby. K.C. is a little closer to the edge of his personal envelope tonight. When a couple turns into the restaurant behind us, he snaps at them, "If you don't eat all your food, bring a doggy bag for us." . . .

A block away I cross paths with two guys standing out of the rain under the overhang of a closed lunch stand. Both in their twenties, one white, the other black. It quickly becomes apparent that all they have in common is this dry spot of sidewalk. The white guy, who tells me his name is Wayne, asks me for some change, telling me he got laid off from a construction job. The black guy, without introducing himself, quickly tries to take over. "Hey, I'm in a situation too. I'm a starving artist, and nobody's giving me nothing. I don't have a job. But I'm a millionaire, I know that inside. That my art is worth money, OK? But I know I'm gonna make it. All I got to do is go to New York. I've been trying for four years to get back there. I just need enough money to go to New York. The only thing I need is like 150 bucks."

I ask him if he ever tries finding work in the want ads. "Everybody keeps saying that, man! The paper is to get you to buy it or look at it. They're still making money off you! Hey, see all these stores out here? Every one of them got a loan to get what they've got. Well, I need a loan. If I had a loan for about $10,000, I'd be a multimillionaire, man. . . .

Wayne hasn't said a word during this rap. But when the starving artist, now pretty agitated, nervously walks to the corner to search out better possibilities than me, Wayne rolls his eyes and says to me out of the corner of his mouth, "It don't take nobody no four years to get back to New York, I'm sorry." Wayne is not wildly drunk, but now that I'm standing close to him I can tell he's pretty numbed up. Wayne is one of the truly unsheltered homeless. In good weather he sleeps in the park just opposite the Q street Metro exit. In bad weather he sleeps under the portico of an attorney's office or in a nearby building that's under construction. He has shoulder-length light-blond hair coming down from under his ball cap, a moustache, and the beginnings of a beard. About four years ago, he came to this area from Texas with his family. Then his mother died and his father started a housepainting company in Virginia. Wayne used to work there. I ask him why he quit. This was, after all, the decision that finally put him on the street. I figure there had to be a pretty dramatic reason. All Wayne comes up with is this: "I just couldn't deal with it, too many Spanish workers—they can't speak English because most of them are illegal immigrants—and being the boss's son."

The artist comes back. "Can you give me a buck or 50 cents, man, so I can get on the subway?" he asks me. As I give him two quarters, I notice that he's wearing a Burberry scarf. After he leaves, Wayne says, "I don't like him. He's a con artist. I'm watching right now to see if he gets on the subway." He doesn't.

Wayne turns his attention back to me. "I used to be in trouble all the time until I got my head cleared. Put it this way," he chuckles, "I got a few tatoos from prison." Wayne says his conviction for knifing a guy in a Texas bar fight is a problem when he's looking for work. "That's why I go for jobs that are under the table."

Hope for Some Homeless

In my travels around Washington, I rarely see homeless women on the street. But there are places outdoors where they congregate. One such spot is a steep stretch of Belmont Street in the northwest quadrant of the city. Walking north on 14th Street and turning onto Belmont any evening at around 5:30, you will gradually become aware of a pilgrimage—first just a few shadows moving through the uneven light, but eventually a line of them making the daily trek up to the top of the hill. Most of the shadows are families, virtually all black, living in temporary housing for the homeless. There are very few men, either by themselves or attached to a family group. I fall in step with the shadow families, curious to see what could have this drawing power.

At the top of the hill is the one-time Pitts Hotel, a ramshackle building now operated as a shelter for homeless families. Parked out front under the archway is a gleaming yellow Rolls Royce, District license plate 347. A man standing next to it tells me that it belongs to the building's owner, Cornelius Pitts. The people file by it without taking much notice. The building has room for only 50 or so families, but every day the District's Department of Human Services deposits four additional busloads of shelter residents—mostly families—at the foot of the hill so that they can get a cooked meal.

Watching the women come and go on Belmont, you can't avoid the feeling that they are fighting some powerful obstacles in addition to the lack of a permanent place to live. Many seem tired and cranky, snapping at their children and cuffing them for transgressions that are hard to see in this light. "I'm not here because I'm all drugged up," says a plump woman with four kids in tow, hurrying down the hill to make the last bus. "I work as a nurse's assistant at D.C. General, and the truth is"—her voice lowers—"I had to leave where I was living because my friend was beating on me."

Despite these dark overtones, the longer I watch and listen, the more I become aware of the many hopeful signs on Belmont Street. As a group, these women seem fairly straight. Straight enough for Tom Brokaw. They stand in stark contrast to street hustlers like K.C. or the artist. Although the meals and the pickup buses run on such a tight schedule that most of the women are in too much of a hurry to talk to me, those who do tell me that they are working, leaving their kids with babysitters during the day. A gregarious teenage mother of an 11-month-old tells me her biggest complaint: these daily crosstown voyages for food have left her baby with a persistent cold. A soft-spoken woman with three kids tells me that she has just gotten herself on a list downtown for housing placement; she hopes that in a few more weeks the city will be able to locate a place for her. Most of the women are dressed neatly, and some of the kids are in adorable get-ups: Bows in hair and party shoes for the girls, superhero jackets and team ballcaps for the boys. Obviously, many of these people are using their meager means for the right things; given more sustenance, most of them would only do more of the same. Yes, for the Belmont families, it seems that housing *would* be a big part of the answer.

Heartbreak Hotel

At Mt. Carmel House, a homeless women's shelter in Washington's Chinatown, you can meet the people the Belmont Street women are trying not to become. Ann, for instance—a sad-eyed 41-year-old black woman who has come to this women's shelter straight from a stint at the detox unit at D.C. General. Ann discovered she couldn't handle alcohol after many years of what she calls "trial and error." Before booze derailed her life, she was a data clerk at the Veterans' Administration. But now she's lost her job, and her 18-year-old daughter lives with Ann's mother.

Or there's Marsha, a black woman in her twenties whose five years on cocaine and one year of living on the streets have somehow left her eyeballs and her teeth the same yellow color. This time last year, she was pawning anything she could get her hands on and working as a prostitute to raise drug money. A high-school dropout who was sexually abused by her father, Marsha has a daughter by a man she used to live with; she no longer has any contact with him and the authorities have taken the child away. Last November, Marsha got shot in the head by "some crackhead going around in the streets shooting for the hell of it. I should have gone to the doctor right away," she says. "But I wouldn't go to the doctor until I'd done all my cocaine first."

Celeste Valente, who's been a social worker at Mt. Carmel House for eight years, says that the shelter's 40-odd resident population now includes more younger women than it used to. There's been a decrease in the mentally ill clientele (now 30 percent of the population, down from 80 percent a few years ago) and an increase in drug addicts (almost all those in the shelter who are not mentally ill are substance abusers). Valente guesses that "more than 80 percent of the women who come here have been raped or were the victims of incest."

Another woman living at Mt. Carmel is Virginia, who's spent the last year in shelters—four in all. She's white, in her forties, with "done" hair, pink lipstick, and rouged cheeks. Her handbag says "Maui" on it. She could easily pass for a suburbanite down here doing volunteer work. In fact, she now volunteers a couple of nights a week at a nearby dinner program. "When I was working," Virginia remembers, "I gave about $1,500 of my United Way funds to the House of Ruth [another women's shelter in Washington]. And when I became homeless, that's the first place I went." Virginia's father was career Army. She was born in Austria. She has a literature degree from Georgetown. "I had the life," she says.

Here it seems I've come across a person worthy of Jonathan Kozol, the Salvation Army, and all the other "it could happen to anyone" theorists. But there's a difference they might not like. Virginia's an alcoholic. And she spent a long time in what she describes as a "sick" relationship with a sexually abusive man. After she was laid off from her job managing an engineering office, she stayed in her apartment, watched TV, and drank for eight months. "I drank copious amounts of beer," she tells me, "three six-packs to a case a day."

Karmic Crossed Wires

During the eighties, Lafayette Park, just across Pennsylvania Avenue from the White House, became a campground for homeless squatters. Indeed, some people have lived there for most of the decade, conducting what they call a "peace vigil." The vigil is often on the itinerary of school classes visiting from out of town. The peace squatters have positioned themselves along the south edge of the park, where their placards about Hiroshima and nuclear freeze face the president's front door. Sixties-like, they give themselves new names like "Sunrise." One vigiler I talk to, who's lived here for three years, used to work as an art restorer before joining the scene he describes as a "karmic crossfire." He doesn't want to live anywhere else. He supports himself by performing three nights a week in a "folk rock" band. The rest of the time he's out in the park, sometimes sleeping in his jury-rigged plastic shelter, sometimes cooking up a stew, or greeting pedestrians with lines like, "Peace, brother. Thanks for smiling"—whether the guy is smiling or not.

But some of the homeless in Lafayette Park are conducting more private vigils. Take the man on the park bench, hands on knees, open bottle of beer at his feet, just staring intensely at the White House. With the green of his poncho and the way his eyes are bulging, he looks like a frog on a lily pad. "I'm here to talk to

George," he tells me. When he sees my fatigue pants, he goes to Red Alert, "Are you Marine Corps, FBI, Secret Service? Are you wearing a tape recorder?" I reassure him. He's so close to jumping out of his skin that I worry about what would happen if he were to notice the two men in uniform on the White House roof. "Yeah, George is a good man," the guy on the bench says, continuing to stare straight ahead. "I don't have nothing against him. He's a naval aviator and all that. When he went out to San Francisco after that earthquake, I talked to him." I asked the man if he flew out there to do that. "Nope," he says, never taking his eyes off his quarry, "talked to him by Telstar."

The Telstar man has plenty of company in Washington. Near my office for instance, there is the tall, helmeted man who keeps a guardpost at the corner of Q and Connecticut. When you get close to him, you can see that he's wearing a flannel West German army uniform. He's sort of handsome and he has that straight-from-the-diaphragm voice and ramrod posture so valued in drill instructors. His long reddish brown hair runs in a thin, tight braid down his back. Tucked in his helmet and pointing straight up are three toothbrushes, looking like periscopes.

When I ask him his name, he replies, "General. U.S. General. None of that Noriega thing for me." I notice that he's wearing a Top Gun squadron patch; he tells me where he got it: "The Surgeon General distributed it to the field artillery and ballistics command and the dominions of trade. Top Gun. Miramar California. I took the training out there about eight weeks ago. It was about the failure to inform people at the White House. And to maintain gun standards, computer standards, or surgical standards."

When I ask General what he's doing at this corner, he tells me, "This is the field marshal air combat warning post here for the businesses and the banks. This post is the way that the military has become involved about the levering of the topmost business developments." What's he watching out for? The answer comes back instantly: "The Turks." As to how long he'll be in this assignment, General guesses about 40 years. "It should improve sometime in the nineties as far as the Motorola business is concerned. Eventually I will tend towards Walkman business. How the General maintains his districting or vector businesses is highly dependent upon Walkman skills."

General does not know he's homeless. When I ask him where he goes at night and in bad weather, he tells me that he confers with the president. He readily distinguishes himself from pan-handlers, whom he dismisses as "people who have no ownership interests or no mortgage or paper interests." However, in a way, he does have his own version of "Spare some change?" As I'm leaving, he says to me, "You should bring me a banknote so that the interests you represent can be represented here."

The Grate Society

Under an overpass in Foggy Bottom just east of the Potomac and just north of the exclusive Watergate apartment complex are some steam grates that have long served as a thermal oasis for the homeless. The night I walk by is chilly, so the grates are pretty full. When I approach, several of the men there ask me for change. The hot air rushing out of this hole in the ground pro-duces a loud hum you have to shout over. The steam itself pro-vides a two-part sensation: first your face gets hit by a pleasant rush of warmth, then your nose gets hit by the stench of stale booze. Booze that's soaked through clothes, that's soaked through skin, that's soaked through lives.

There are nine or ten men at the grate this night. It's an in-terracial group. Some are huddled at the edges, some just racked out across it. The two men who asked me for money talk to me a lot, but some of the others never even look in my direction.

One man tells me he's been out here for two years, another says eight. The liveliest talker is a young black guy named Tony. In his mid-twenties, he's handsome and, in an alcoholic sort of way, articulate. Tony points to a woman coming our way. "Here comes my girlfriend. That's why I'm out here, because of her." A black woman weaves towards us. She's really drunk. She plops down sullenly at the edge of the grate, no use for anybody. "I met her in July when I came out the Navy," Tony says, unaccountably thrilled to see her.

Tony says he's not really homeless because he can stay with his aunt at 14th and Euclid. But it's real late and he's still out here drinking.

Tony says he was in the Navy for eight years. "Aviation. Back-seater in F-14s. I was a second lieutenant. I worked in the Indian Ocean on the *Nimitz*. Just got out in July. I'm going back. I'm in the reserves." There's a pause. "I was supposed to been back—I'm not going to lie to you. I'm AWOL [absent without leave]. When I came out of high school and went to the Navy, I started out as an

NCO—a noncommissioned officer. I was an NCO all the way. I went to school in Annapolis. When I go back, they may drop me down to like E-4. After I get out of the brig. I see Navy cars go by here every day. They're MPs, man, I know they lookin' for me.

"I want to re-up for maybe four more years. And then come back and get me a job at one of these airports as an aviator or air traffic controller. But it's gonna be a while for me now because last Saturday night, some girl stabbed me in my chest. And all I got is one lung now." As he's telling me this, Tony's unbuttoning his shirt. He shows me a Band-Aid just under his clavicle. It's not a very elaborate dressing, and I don't see any signs of actual injury. "I just got out of the hospital. And today two guys tried to jump on me." Tony shows me his punching hand. The knuckles on it are very swollen. "So it's gonna be a while—maybe another two months—until I go back."

Tony says the Navy sent him here on shore leave to bury his grandmother. "That's when I met Karen," he tells me, nodding toward the poor woman who just joined us. "Took a liking to her. And she turned my head around." He says Karen used to drive trucks in the Army, that she was in Vietnam. He says she's 38. She looks 58. Tony reaches between his knees into the red plastic milk crate he's sitting on and pulls out a white plastic flask. Gin, he tells me. A pint a day. Pointing at the others, he explains, "They drink that hard stuff."

Tony's story was fascinating, but it wasn't true. You can't start out in the service as an NCO, and "second lieutenant" is not a rank in the Navy.

The old man at my feet, whom Tony introduces as Jimmy, "the granddaddy of the grates," mumbles at me. In the slurred words of a lifelong drunk he tells me that he's worked as a tow-truck driver at an Amoco station for 18 years. But, he says, "See those," pointing at some of Georgetown's poshest apartments, "I don't make enough money to rent no apartment for $250 a month. So I stay here." Jimmy's incredibly dirty. He never looks up at me. His attention is riveted on a little pack of picture cards he keeps riffling through. They're not baseball cards, although they're that size. Because they're predominantly pink, I assume they're pornographic. When Jimmy hands me one, I see they're not. They're pictures of food. The card in my hand is "Shrimp with Greens."

The closest thing to an American monument to homelessness

is the shelter run by the Community for Creative Non-Violence (CCNV) in the former Federal City College building at the intersection of 2nd and D in downtown Washington. This is the building that the federal government agreed to lease to homeless advocate Mitch Snyder in 1984 after Snyder led a 51-day fast. Housing 1,400 homeless—1,265 men and 135 women—it's the largest shelter in the country, perhaps in the world. CCNV's literature calls it "a national model."

Since its inception, the CCNV shelter has received over $13 million in combined federal and D.C. appropriations, and another $500,000 in corporate donations. I wanted to get an idea of what that money is buying. To do that, I decided to take my idea of talking to the homeless one step further by going to the shelter and asking for help.

Shelter Skelter

I showed up at CCNV late on a Saturday afternoon in January, dressed in my worst clothes and having not washed or shaved for days. In front of the building, Saturday night is already well underway. Thirty or so men are standing on the porch and along the sidewalk, talking loudly and taking regular pulls from the brown paper bags they all seem to have. One of the louder guys is a gapped-toothed man in a purple parka. He's shouting out at anybody walking by and going through a loud review of the lunch he had at some soup kitchen: "Uhhhh-uhhhh, barbecue chicken! I'm telling you, they got *down*. . . ."

When they're not drinking and cursing, the men spend a lot of time spitting. The sidewalk is phlegm-spotted. It's hard to find a dry spot on the steps to sit on. Almost as soon as I do, I attract the attention of a disastrously drunk man who until then had been working full-time trying to keep from impacting the sidewalk. He's lurching about furiously, like a man on the deck of a storm-blown ship. He finally makes it over next to me. Even sitting down, he's weaving. He mumbles something to me I can't make out. The second time, I catch it: "Do you have five cents?" When I say I don't, he repeats the question. Then he mumbles something else, "What's in the bag?" For authenticity, I have a paper bag with me. The drunk grabs my arm and tries to pull me towards him. "What's in the bag?" "Nothing for you," I tell him, moving away. . . .

When a woman comes to the front of the building with some

stuff to donate, Purple Parka comes down and swarms all over
her, putting his arm around her and trying to take her through a
door where she doesn't want to go. "Be sociable," another man
tells him. "You not on the staff." Parka snaps back, "I ain't yo'
nigger." When a girl with a pretty hairstyle walks by, he shouts at
her, "I want your hair!" She replies, "You gonna buy me some
more?"

I move down to the wooden benches near one corner of the
building. From here, I can see something that I couldn't before.
Behind a van across the street, two guys are fighting. They must
be pretty drunk; the pace doesn't let up a bit even when one guy
slams the other's head into the van.

There's a constant stream of men coming in and out of the
building. A beer can in a paper sack is practically part of the
uniform. A few weeks before tonight, *Newsweek* ran a picture of
the area where I'm sitting now. In the shot, the CCNV building
and grounds looked spic-and-span. The three guys now on the
bench to my right, sharing a joint, weren't there. And neither
were the two women and one guy on the sidewalk right in front of
me, passing a reefer between them. A young black guy dressed in
the immaculate fashion of followers of Muslim leader Louis Far-
rakhan—black suit, bow tie, highly polished shoes—comes over
to the trio. I expect him to tell them to put the joint out. But
instead he takes off his Walkman and lends it to one of the wom-
en. She closes her eyes and sways to the music, continuing to take
her tokes. . . .

So far, out of the hundred or so people I've seen at CCNV,
I'm the only white. That's why I notice when three white guys
come out of the building. They're walking down the ramp when
a tall man with one of those Eraserhead hairdos that's high and
flat on top and shaved bald all around the sides suddenly comes
up in their faces and edges them towards the wall. He says something to them and then they sheepishly continue on their way.
Eraserhead has now joined Purple Parka out front as one of
CCNV's unofficial greeters. He's got a pocket square tucked
into his sports jacket, and is wearing a fancy-looking watch and
four rings.

I go inside to find out what prospects there are for getting put
up for the night. I'm told that the shelter is full until Tuesday, but
that a van will eventually come to take me to one of the city's
emergency shelters. I decide to wait in the lobby. Over the next
couple of hours there I see a lot.

Residents continue to stream in and out of the building. (There is no sign-in or sign-out. The building is open most of the time. Between midnight and 4 a.m. the front door is opened for five minutes every half hour.) About a third of the people I see are carrying Walkman sets. At least half are carrying beer or liquor. The stuff's usually in a paper bag, but several people, Eraserhead among them, are carrying beer in plastic cups. Later, a CCNV spokesman named Lawrence Lyles tells me that CCNV policy is that "we allow people to have beer and hard stuff, but not illegal drugs. As long as they maintain themselves. This is the residents' house. If you were home, you'd drink a little beer, wouldn't you?" But more than a few of the residents are not maintaining themselves. Drunks—weaving, falling-down drunks—are a common sight in the lobby. Some of them get up the steps only because they are carried up. Only once does a staff member ask anybody what he's carrying in. And when the resident laughs off the question, the staff member doesn't pursue it. What I see supports what an experienced city social worker tells me later: "There are drugs in CCNV. The place is out of control."

Conversation here tends to be animated, often hostile. "If all you needed to live was a teaspoon of water," one man snaps at another, "I wouldn't give it to you." Another man explains in a loud voice why he wants a stiletto. "Because if I miss you one way, I'll cut you coming back." "Look," says one laughing guy to his friend, pointing to a bearded, wasted white man whose eyes are set on infinite, "Charlie Manson is on parole."

A handsome man with longish gray-black hair comes down to get his mail. He's carrying two books, the first I've seen here. He's neatly dressed in a completely coordinated Army camouflage uniform. In this scene, he looks as solid as a rock. He's walking towards me as he finishes his letter. "They say they will give me money if I go to a psychiatrist," he tells me, his face lit up now by a scary smile. "But I will stay here instead!"

Even in this chaos, there are some touches fit for a public service announcement. An older black man asks a feeble-looking white man about how he's mending since he got hit by a car. He listens patiently as the man shows him his injuries and explains what medical appointments he has set up in the days ahead. A lady gives a man in a wheelchair a spin he clearly enjoys.

At about 8 p.m., one of the staff members very politely informs the few of us who've been waiting for transportation that there will be no van run tonight. He quickly goes on to tell us that there's room at one of the city's newest emergency shelters. And it's within walking distance, over at the Department of Employment Services [DES] just around the corner.

On my way there, I fall in with two other guys, Tom and James, headed for the same place. They are both refreshingly clean-cut and substance-free. We all shake hands and quickly hit it off. The DES shelter is actually in the employees' parking garage underneath the building. It's well heated, and the nice lady volunteer who checks us in issues us like-new Army cots and a tuna sandwich apiece. There are about 50 people already on cots when we arrive—the place is full. The three of us help each other set up our cots. Tom takes a shower and brings some cups and water back from the bathroom to make up some Kool-Aid he's brought with him. He shares it with James and me and gives us each a cookie, too. The shelter atmosphere is pretty much like that of a barracks; there's plenty of "smokin' and jokin'" but the drunks are mostly down for the count. The roving armed guard probably helps.

The three of us talk among ourselves. Tom's a white guy with a bushy moustache. He just got out of jail—during a routine traffic stop the day before, he got arrested on an old warrant for driving without a license. He made bail, but he's from Virginia, and without a license or car (it got impounded), and low on money, he has no way to get back. And he has no place to stay here. His court date is next month, and he figures he will get some jail because, as he puts it, "this isn't the first time."

James is black and works in the kitchen at the Marriott in Crystal City. He's wearing an Army jacket, from his days as a parachute rigger in the Airborne. This is his first day on the streets. He had been living with his girlfriend, but they had a fight. James works on the side as a party DJ. At one of these parties, a girl gave him her phone number to give to a friend of his, but James's girlfriend discovered it in his jacket and went nuts, throwing James out of the house and all of his stuff down the stairs. I ask James if there isn't a family member he can stay with until this boils over. "I tried staying with my mother," he answers, "but she had too many restrictions—she won't give me a key, she won't let me in past 11 at night, and there's no TV downstairs. I'm a party animal."

Lying back on my cot, I spend a long time staring at the garage ceiling, trying to figure out James's logic. Why would somebody clean and employed choose this—and tomorrow night maybe something much worse—over coming in at 11 to a house with only one TV? Would "people you know" do that?

Conspicuous Dysfunction

The Depression taught most Americans that there are plenty of ways to become poor that aren't one's fault. By now this is a lesson well learned. Perhaps too well-learned. Americans tend to believe that homelessness is exclusively a social problem, a system failure. This idea goes hand-in-hand with the traditional liberal notion that the solution to the problem is simply the provision of housing and jobs. While there is something to this, it's not *the* solution—as I found out for myself there's too much else going on with the homeless.

Allowing for the possibility of some overlap, here's how I would roughly classify the homeless people I met: At least three-quarters were (current or recovering) substance abusers, three-quarters were unattached men, and about a third seemed to some degree mentally ill. But there is another important factor I observed in about half of the homeless people I talked to—one that takes a little explaining. I call it the "X-factor" because I'm not having much luck figuring it out. [Footnote: It's interesting to compare my description of the homeless population based on my own experience with what you can find in print elsewhere. Most respected policy studies and surveys are now saying that about a third of the homeless are mentally ill, a third are substance abusers, and a third are "other." That is, they find less substance abuse than I did, about the same amount of mental illness, and tend to leave the rest of the population an undifferentiated mystery while I think some of that remainder is in the grip of X-factor thinking.]

Ronald Reagan once came in for a lot of well-deserved criticism for saying that anybody who is homeless is so only because he chooses to be. That's a ridiculous notion. Sleeping in the park in the winter, being chronically sick and disoriented—nobody chooses *that*. But just the same, people like the New York artist, Wayne from Texas, and James are carrying something around in their heads that's separating them from opportunities and propelling them towards ruin. The artist has his incoherent put-down of the classifieds, Wayne has his equally confused contempt for the work at his father's business, and James has his odd standards about acceptable living conditions. Here are some other examples of the X-factor I came across in talking to the homeless:

• One of the beggars I frequently see is a 24-year-old black guy who goes by the street name "Quickness." He can usually be found around Dupont Circle either zoned out or trying to be. He tells me that he originally came to Washington to sell PCP, but he got caught and spent three years in jail. He's been on the streets for the seven months since he got out. When I ask him what he wants out of life, he tells me "money." His parents are back in Florida, and they know he's up here, but he won't go back to them and he won't even tell them he's homeless. Quickness prefers staying in the streets to that.

• A fiftyish man whom I often see late at night begging near my office, an articulate man who appears sane and drug- and alcohol-free, tells me that he served in submarines in the Navy and then worked at the Nuclear Regulatory Commission. He says that he lost his job at the NRC because of differences with his bosses. Later, he landed a job stuffing envelopes for a political organization, but he quit because he didn't agree with the material he was mailing and went back to the streets, where he makes about $2 an hour (it turns out that's the typical figure for a Washington beggar).

• A young woman I met who splits her begging between Dupont Circle and Georgetown tells me that she recently failed the Civil Service exam. I ask her if she has tried to get into a job training program. "I feel that I don't have the time for that. I just want something right now. Something I can just walk into and get right then and there."

All of these people fail the Bill Shade test. Bill is the only single male homeless person I met who I am convinced is actively trying every day to become unhomeless. Bill was working in construction when he got burned out of his apartment. Most of what Bill collects from begging he turns over to the woman who takes care of his daughter. Once I was talking to Bill when I noticed the Help Wanted sign behind his head. He read my mind: "I already went in there, but they want a girl to work behind the counter." So instead he sweeps the sidewalk in front of the shop. He works odd jobs whenever he can. He cleans up around the bank where he sleeps. He puts quarters in expired parking meters to save people he doesn't know from paying the $15 ticket. He's hoping to get the funds together to move back to Baltimore with his daughter.

If reading this story makes you feel like helping a single homeless person directly, call me or write me about Bill Shade.

I'm finding it hard to articulate the troublesome mental baggage that hampers the New York artist or Quickness say, but not Bill Shade. It's not, contra the Reagan camp, mere laziness—these people work much harder every day than most just to keep from freezing to death. It's something more like a twisted sense of pride—a sense of personal specialness tweaked so ridiculously high that anything—even sleeping outside and begging for food—is viewed as better than forms of compromise that you and I would readily accept, like fitting in at work, getting a job out of the newspaper, or coming home at 11. For all I can tell, some of this odd thinking is the extreme rationalization so common in alcoholics and substance abusers, and some is a sign of a treatable organic thought disorder, like mild schizophrenia. But I'm also convinced that some of the homeless I met who evinced the X-factor were neither mentally ill nor addicts. What do we make of them?

If you've raised children in the seventies and eighties, then you know how the emphasis on rampant instant gratification and conspicuous consumption of such television fare as "Dallas," "Lifestyles of the Rich & Famous," and "L.A. Law" can distort your children's desires and expectations. Sometimes being "tough"—emphasizing setting goals and working hard to achieve them, etc.—brings kids around on this. But many parents have experienced the bewilderment that comes when that doesn't work. How do we reach Johnny? How do we bring him down to earth so that he can make a good life for himself? Parents can use up a decade or more wrestling with such questions, often without arriving at an answer. Well, maybe the bewilderment I feel in the face of the foregoing examples is similar, with a similar cause. But about two or three times more extreme. It seems that some of the homeless have just soaked up way too much of our culture's obsession with "too much, too soon."

There can be all the low-cost housing in the world, and an untreated paranoid won't set foot in it, and an untreated schizophrenic might burn it down. (Dr. E. Fuller Torrey, a psychiatrist who is an expert on the homeless mentally ill, told me that he has encountered both outcomes.) And a drug addict will spend the rent money on crack. So homelessness is in large measure a mental health problem and a drug problem that defies the conventional liberal answers of housing and jobs. But notice this about the X-factor homeless: They aren't likely to be people for whom jobs and housing alone would be the answer, either. Once a man decides to eat only caviar, he will turn down bread as fervently as an ordinary man turns down poison. If low cost housing were made available to the New York artist (and for all I know, it already has been), but there was no $10,000 loan, how would he pay the rent? If he were offered a nonglamorous job to make the rent, would he take it?

There certainly seem to be homeless people who are nearly like you and me, save for some intervening bad breaks. Many of the women on Belmont Street appear to fit that bill, as does Bill Shade. So for people like these, fixing the bad break—making jobs and housing available—*is* what's called for. But media depictions to the contrary, there are more homeless people—the untreated mentally ill, the addicted, and those with the X-factor—*who are not like us*. As a result, if they are ever to realize secure and steady lives, they will require different kinds of help.

Traditional liberals don't want to admit such differences—and that's wrong—because they want us to help all the homeless—that's right. Neoconservatives admit the differences (right) because they don't want to help them all (wrong). The correct position is to admit the differences among the homeless while strenuously working to help them all. If conservatives need to care more, liberals need to *see* more. It's a cruel joke to pretend that an untreated mentally ill person is better off in the streets than he would be if he were compelled somehow to take medication, or to pretend that Quickness would hold down a job with the same tenacity as Bill Shade. To make real progress in the fight against homelessness, we must first be honest about who the homeless are.

THE HIDDEN HOMELESS: DOWN AND OUT IN SUBURBIA[3]

Elmsford, New York
"I never thought I'd be living in a Howard Johnson's," Roger Jones is telling me one bright morning in May while he looks out

[3]Article by Brad Kessler, from *The Nation* 249:306 S 25 '89. Copyright © 1989 by The Nation Company, Inc. Reprinted with permission.

his picture window at a perfect Westchester County spring—the forsythia bushes in full bloom, the wooded hills, carpeted and kelly green, rolling westward out to the Hudson River. Roger is a black man in his late 20s who is dressed in sneakers and a windbreaker and has the clean-cut looks of a prep-school graduate. Married and with kids, he grew up in Elmsford, went to college, worked briefly on Wall Street and lived in Washington, D.C., before returning to his native Westchester. When he came back two years ago to the place that real estate developers like to call "Country Club Country" he couldn't find an affordable place to live and ended up, like thousands of others here, homeless.

I'm talking with Roger (not his real name) this morning at the Elmsford Motor Lodge. The motel was once, in a happier age, a Howard Johnson's, and there are still reminders of its HoJo past—the orange plastic pantiles, the robin's-egg-blue spire, the A-frame entrance hall. But the restaurant is now boarded up and the name has changed. The hallways are full of trash; the sounds of soap operas and children crying come from behind the closed doors, and ever since the motel became a kind of holding pen for a hundred of Westchester's homeless families, nobody here thinks about getting HoJo hotcakes in the morning or service with a smile.

Westchester County is not the type of place people think of when they talk about the homeless. Forty minutes north of New York City, it unfolds with sylvan parkways, lush corporate parks and towns with Anglican names like Ardsley and Irvington, where the average house sells for $300,000 and is probably within putting distance of a golf course or tennis court. The typical Westchester household has an income of more than $40,000 a year, and even in the more blue-collar towns like Elmsford, Sybaris is never too far away: Right up the road from the Elmsford Motor Lodge live the Rockefellers on the 3,000-acre fiefdom their grandfather built; a little farther east, down Route 287, the corporate parks of "Platinum Mile" float above the verdure of Westchester Avenue like a topographic rendering of the Fortune 500 list—Texaco, Pepsico and International Paper, to name but a few. It's not surprising, then, that Westchester was home to the first golf course ever built in the New World, the first shopping mall and (as legend holds) the first cocktail. Yet now it has another superlative to add to its list, for Westchester today leads the nation in homeless people per capita.

[In 1989] there were 4,200 homeless people in Westchester,

most of them in families and among them 1,710 children. The majority became homeless because of what the Westchester Department of Social Services calls "economic reasons," which means they couldn't pay the rising rents, or were forced out of their apartments because of co-op conversion or gentrification. Some were burned out of their apartments or crowded out of public housing. All of them simply couldn't find another place to live because, as Roger Jones puts it, "Finding an affordable apartment in Westchester is like trying to thread a needle with a Mack truck."

Today just about every town in Country Club Country has its own story of native homelessness, even the matronly, mock-Tudor towns of Scarsdale and New Rochelle—the very symbols of Northeastern wealth. But to see the homeless in Westchester as something aberrant or contradictory is to miss the point entirely. Homelessness exists here *because* Westchester is one of the wealthiest counties in the country. Professionals who moved out of the city for a piece of Arcadia have been displacing poorer Westchester residents for decades. But in the Reagan years, the county's exorbitant housing costs spiraled upward and left even less room for those whose incomes corkscrewed downward at the same time. Unlike in the cities, homelessness in the suburbs is a diffuse matter. There is no central authority in a place like Westchester at which to point the finger of blame. Instead, responsibility is dissipated among village, town, county and state governments. The homeless themselves are thinly spread throughout the county, between vast suburban spaces, making them virtually invisible.

Michelle Altro is fairly typical of Westchester's homeless. Like Roger Jones, she lives at the Elmsford Motor Lodge, and has been there for eight months. She is 19 years old, white, dressed in acid-washed jeans and wears glasses with rose-colored rims. She's been living in the motel with her 10-month-old baby ever since her landlord kicked her out of her one-bedroom apartment in Ossining when he decided he didn't want infants living there. Michelle works at the nearby Sizzler for $4.75 an hour. The money's not great, but it's one of the few places that will hire you if you live in a motel. With the money she makes, and with the help of Section 8 funds [from the Housing and Community Development Act of 1974, which provided landlords with difference between a low-income tenant's rent and 30% of his or her income], she can afford to pay as much as $300 a month for an apartment for herself and her infant. But nowhere in Westchester can she find an apartment at that rent, and neither can the various agencies, including Social Services and private organizations, that are looking for her.

Michelle can pretty much deal with life in the motel, with the maids who steal her medication and her baby's stuffed animals, with the addicts who smoke crack in the bathroom upstairs and whose clouds of cocaine smoke blow down through the vents into her apartment. She can deal with doors slamming around her at all hours of the night, with having nowhere to cook a hot meal, with being charged $5 by motel security just to have her door opened when she forgets her key. But the bugs are another thing entirely. It's not the cockroaches that she minds so much—although she leaves the lights on at night to keep them away—it's the ants, the biting kind, the ones that crawl up the legs of her baby's crib and get to its face, its eyes, its nostrils.

If you become homeless in Country Club Country, you'll probably end up at a motel like the Elmsford Motor Lodge or at any other of Westchester's forty-odd available motels. Your chances are one in five of being placed out of county, since Westchester does not have enough motel rooms to shelter all its homeless. You may be placed as far as eighty miles from your former home, in a motel near the Pennsylvania border, or be deported upstate to Poughkeepsie or Newburgh, where your children may be shipped back and forth from their school to the motel, on a two-hour ride twice a day. The county will pay the cab fare, which can run as much as $220 round-trip, but it will not pay for adults to travel to and from a job that they may have left eighty miles behind, in Yonkers or New Rochelle.

Many of the motels used for homeless people violate basic health, fire and safety regulations. The Fox Ridge Motor Inn in neighboring Putnam County, which housed twenty-three homeless families sent up from Westchester, was closed down in April by the State Supreme Court because it violated sanitary codes. In a typical motel as many as four people live in a room meant to accommodate an overnighting couple. Crime and drugs are the rule. People who live in the Elmsford Motor Lodge, for example, say that more than 80 percent of the residents use crack. Lestor Trebony, who runs the County Center Motel in White Plains, says that several of his residents became addicted to crack after they moved into the motel. "You get people coming in here that are so nice at the beginning," says Diane Schultz, who lives in the

Elmsford Motor Lodge. "But by the time they leave here, they're drug addicts or they're so bitter because this place just makes them crazy. And then nobody will rent you an apartment once they find out you've been living in a motel."

When you visit a place like the Elmsford Motor Lodge, it is hard not to think of other forms of housing meant to contain a population rather than merely shelter it: Internment camps come to mind, as do model villages or strategic hamlets. Security guards watch the grounds with cameras and patrol the motel with walkie-talkies. Visiting hours are 8 in the morning to 10 at night, after which no one is admitted if he or she doesn't belong.

Most of the homeless motels in Westchester serve not only to contain the homeless people but also to conceal them from the outside world. The Elmsford Motor Lodge, the Parkway Motel, the Coachman Hotel and the Larchmont Motel, to name a few, are conveniently situated away from residential areas, along access routes or abandoned stretches of downtown. The Elmsford Motor Lodge is located on a wooded ridge, invisible to those driving by on Tarrytown Road. A few miles away, the Parkway Motel is similarly tucked away, in a wooded corner along the Saw Mill River Parkway so that the only people who can see it are motorists speeding by. The people who live in the motels feel they are being hidden and speak often of their isolation, of having nowhere to go, nothing to do. Placed in an alien, often hostile community, they stay inside their rooms and rarely go out. Even people who have lived in the motels for more than a year say they have little or no contact with the surrounding neighborhoods. And so the motels have become suburban ghettos, keeping the homeless to themselves—but unlike a ghetto, they are only temporary dwellings. There are no kitchens or living rooms or stoves, no place, no matter how dreary or destitute, they can call home.

To put a homeless family up in a one-bedroom motel unit, Westchester County pays an average rent of $3,000 a month. This is good business for the motel owners, and the local cab companies that transport the homeless to far-flung destinations are also enjoying something of a boom. But the irony of their profitability isn't lost on the homeless themselves. "I grew up in Westchester," says Roger Jones, "in a scattered-site public housing project. They were the last low-income housing projects ever built in the county, and that was done fifteen years ago. I want to know why they can't build anything like that anymore. People say they don't want us in their backyards, but we lived here before those people even moved in. I guess people around here would rather pay $3,000 a month to keep us in these motels instead of seeing us have housing."

Some people, as it happens, do mind paying that kind of money for the homeless and would rather see them simply disappear or be given one-way bus tickets to Kansas, as one Westchester resident suggested to me, where housing is a lot cheaper. Articles appear periodically in the local papers decrying the absurdity of Westchester's homeless policy. Even the County Executive, a glad-handing Republican named Andrew O'Rourke, publicly laments the loss of money that could better be spent for other things. "Imagine how much permanent housing $64 million could build," he wrote recently in a letter to *The New York Times*. "Think of the other services—parks, programs for the elderly, the arts, day care—$64 million could buy." And yet, despite O'Rourke's letters and public proclamations, there is a quiet acceptance of the way things are, of keeping the homeless holed up in motel rooms, because the obvious solution of building low-income housing is simply a taboo subject in Country Club Country.

"There is a silence here about the homeless," says County Legislator Paul Feiner, who represents the town of Greenburgh and is one of the county's few self-styled progressives. "People in my district were very pleased when I came out saying let's help the homeless. But when I said I was going to support semipermanent housing, I lost a whole neighborhood. Everybody wants to fund the soup kitchens. You have a lot of churches and synagogues involved in preparing food and going out to feed the homeless, but that only keeps them homeless. Nobody talks about the real issue—building housing—because nobody wants it built. Greenburgh is just a sophisticated Yonkers. The people here don't send their elected officials bullets. They hire lawyers."

Who is responsible, then, for building affordable housing in suburbia? By law, nobody is. New York State law actually prohibits counties from putting up housing, on the premise that decisions as to where and when housing should be built are best left in the hands of local rather than county government. So the county blames towns, villages and cities for not taking the initiative, the state government for prohibiting counties from building housing and the Federal government for slashing the housing budget over the past ten years by some 80 percent. The local governments, for their part, point the finger at one another. "Communities with a significant percentage of low- or moderate-income population say, of course, that they've done their share," says John Nolon, a housing activist and law professor at Westchester's Pace University. "And those that do not have low-income populations say it's not their responsibility. The state is essentially at fault for not defining the responsibility of local governments; they have given no guidance whatsoever." Neither, for that matter, has the Federal government.

It's not that housing isn't being built in Westchester. In the past few years there has been a housing boom in the county; but the kind of housing that has been built is not the kind that many people who have lived in the county for years can afford. While Westchester's old stock of cheaper housing has burned and decayed, nothing has been built to replace it, save for $300,000 condominiums. No one even tries to build low-income housing on any significant scale in Westchester anymore. Some towns in the county, like Harrison and Yorktown, are discovering that their services are suffering because their firemen or police have to live miles away in less expensive communities. These towns have begun to construct housing priced below the market average in order to keep their necessary blue collars nearby.

But when it comes to housing their own poor or currently homeless, it's an entirely different matter. County Executive O'Rourke doesn't even see the need for building low-income housing in Westchester, and thinks that the housing problem will solve itself if "moderate-income" housing is built. "If we could get every community in Westchester to build decent housing for their own policemen and firemen," he told me recently, "we would ameliorate the housing problem. There is a way around the problem without ever asking anyone to build low-income housing in Westchester, because people are just not going to do it here."

And local history bears O'Rourke out, for the citizens of Westchester have consistently tried to block any attempt at building low-income housing in their county in the past few decades. Indeed, from its very inception, Westchester—like so many other affluent American suburbs—was predicated on the principle of exclusion. As early as the late nineteenth century, tenant farmers were being forced off county land as the New York City captains of industry built castles on top of Westchester's wooded hills and dramatically raised property values. Later, restrictive zoning laws kept out of the county what prohibitive prices alone couldn't. By 1980, for example, 99 percent of Westchester's residentially zoned land was reserved exclusively for single-family houses. In certain communities these houses must be surrounded by as much as four acres of land.

In 1972, the State Urban Development Corporation tried to remedy Westchester's desperate lack of low and moderately priced housing stock by implementing its Nine Towns program. The plan would have overridden local zoning ordinances and placed 100 low-income units in each of nine Westchester towns, but community opposition was so strong that the program was taken to court and eventually knocked down as a violation of "home rule." More recently, in 1987, Andrew Cuomo, New York Governor Mario Cuomo's son, proposed building a "transitional" housing facility called HELP II that would temporarily take in some of Westchester's homeless. Cuomo's plan called for the construction of six two-story buildings that would house 108 families in the middle of a thirty-acre wooded site not far from the Elmsford Motor Lodge, in a corner of Greenburgh called May-fair-Knollwood. County Executive O'Rourke would donate county land; the Town Supervisor of Greenburgh, Anthony Veteran, a Democrat, would support the site in his own town; and Cuomo, through his HELP organization, would build the site and, after ten years, hand it over at no cost to the town for it to use in housing the elderly or its municipal employees. On the face of it, Cuomo's plan was the type of small arrangement that satisfied everyone: The taxpayers would pay a little less for housing their homeless, the politicians could say they were doing something to solve the housing crisis, the homeless themselves would have slightly better housing (albeit temporary), and Cuomo himself would reap longer-term political benefits for whatever office he may or may not choose to pursue.

Yet the residents of Knollwood-Mayfair would have none of it. Under the banner of a citizen's group called the Coalition of United Peoples (COUP), they mounted a popular campaign against the project. At one of the many raucous meetings held last year concerning Cuomo's project, hundreds of outraged local citizens showed up to shout down the project's sponsors. Their arguments were familiar enough—the proposed housing would lower property values, increase crime, put a strain on community services. But some were less predictable—that the housing would cut down the growth of precious trees; that parents would be afraid to send their children to the nearby Westchester Community College, and so enrollment would decline; that the project would, according to one resident, "erode not only the environmental quality of the area but the aesthetic and moral as well." One woman said the site was unsuitable because of deer ticks, and when a discussion came up about fire protection of the site, another woman yelled out, "Let it burn."

When the housing project was finally approved by the county, the Mayfair-Knollwood residents decided to secede from the Town of Greenburgh and create their own town, one in which no housing project would be built. The secession movement went to court, where it has been bottled up ever since.

Much has been made of Cuomo's HELP project and the subsequent secession movement, yet the project is not even remotely a solution to Westchester's homeless crisis. While the local media and the Coalition for the Homeless have praised Cuomo for heroically building housing for the homeless, nobody (except, ironically, the citizens of Mayfair-Knollwood) has mentioned the fact that his project is just another stopgap, like the motel rooms, keeping the homeless in a permanently temporary state. In spite of what some Westchester residents may hope, the homeless will not simply disappear from their county or somehow end up in Kansas—bus ticket or not. On the contrary, homelessness is rising at an alarming rate. This means that in the future, Country Club Country will increasingly become, as it already has for thousands, Motel Hell.

HOMELESSNESS: NOW A RURAL PROBLEM,
TOO[4]

Homelessness no longer is just an urban problem, according to an Ohio State University study that points to the growing tide of homeless people in rural areas. It indicates that their numbers have increased about threefold since 1984. The rural homeless are younger and include more women and families with children than do those in large cities.

Since 1984, the number of women among the rural homeless climbed from 32 to 53%. People aged 18–29 who were homeless increased from 47 to 55%. The number of veterans among the rural homeless dropped from 24 to 12% over that period, partly

[4]Article from USA Today (Magazine) 119:3 Ap '91. Copyright © 1991 by The Society for the Advancement of Education. Reprinted with permission.

due to the shift from homeless men to women. Moreover, those who had a history of prior psychiatric hospitalization decreased by about 50%.

The problem of rural homelessness is affected by the shortage of available low-cost housing, indicates Richard First, associate professor of social work. "There isn't a tradition of non-owner housing in rural areas." Also, many rural communities adjacent to urban areas are rezoning available land into developments designed for expensive one-family homes.

"Some counties literally refuse dollars to build Federally subsidized housing units because they don't want the homeless and low-income families in their town," explains Beverly Toomey, professor of social work. Rural communities are not structured to take care of the homeless. Cities have emergency shelters, missions, and other organized efforts to help such people, but relatively poorer rural areas just don't have the resources to provide such services. "These kinds of factors go into why the rural [homeless] problem is growing. It's a terrible blight."

CHILDREN OF POVERTY[5]

It is 9 a.m. on a November morning, and Terrence Quinn, principal of Public School 225 in Rockaway, Queens, New York, is serving breakfast. But he's not in the school cafeteria. He's in the lobby of a ramshackle welfare hotel where homeless parents and their children have come to seek shelter. With a social worker in tow, Quinn has cruised the hotel corridors, knocking on doors, inviting what is an ever-changing group of parents to share coffee and break bagels and doughnuts with him while he tries to persuade them to send their children to his elementary school six blocks—and a world—away.

Quinn first tried his pied piper approach to drawing poor children into his school in November 1988, and he repeats the effort periodically. His aim is to make the parents and children feel welcome in his school. [In 1989,] Jacqueline, a sixth-grader

[5]Article by Sally Reed and R. Craig Sautter, from *Phi Delta Kappan* 71:K1+ Je '90. Copyright © 1990 by Phi Delta Kappa, Inc. Reprinted with permission.

who had lived at the hotel, was selected as the school's valedictorian. One month before the official announcement, she entered Quinn's office and asked to speak to him in private.

"Can someone on welfare actually be the valedictorian?" she asked.

Quinn reassured Jacqueline, a youngster who has overcome many obstacles. Each day millions of others like her are trying to do likewise. And it's not fair. While the last decade became known in the media for its rampant greed, it left millions of poor people (and their children) literally out in the cold. The outcomes are heartbreaking. Why should a child such as Jacqueline feel so humiliated and ashamed of her predicament?

Jacqueline doesn't know it, but she's not alone. We've all been numbed by the horror stories we've heard of late—stories of homeless families sleeping in cars and of crack babies abandoned to hospital nurseries. Meanwhile, the mind-boggling statistics paint a dreadful picture of what life in this nation is like for far too many children. Once you gather all the figures—from conferences, from government agencies, and from scores of reports—the result is frightening. As a nation we're talking about setting goals for fire safety while a wildfire rages out of control all around us. What can educators, politicians, and individual citizens do? People's lives are at stake, and we can't wait any longer.

War Without End

A generation after President Lyndon Johnson declared an official War on Poverty, nearly one-fifth of America's youngest citizens still grow up poor; often sick, hungry, and illiterate; and deprived of safe and adequate housing, of needed social services, and of special educational assistance. Millions of these youngsters are virtually untouched by the vast wealth of the nation in which they begin their fragile and often painful lives.

It didn't take long to lose the War on Poverty. Only a decade after President Johnson's bold declaration, his antipoverty offensive had been lost for millions upon millions of children. By 1975, after the cutback of the Great Society programs by the Nixon and Ford Administrations and after spiraling inflation hit the economy, the interests of children slid lower on the list of economic priorities than even the interests of the elderly. The youngest Americans became the poorest Americans.

During the Great Depression, most Americans were poor. At the end of World War II, about one-third were still poor, but the industrial output of the U.S. was rapidly expanding. By August 1964, when the first antipoverty legislation was enacted, 32 million Americans (about 15% of the population) were materially impoverished. About 13 million of those poor people were children. More of them were elderly.

The one front that has at least received sustained reinforcements since the War on Poverty was scaled back is the fight to improve the lot of the elderly poor. By 1990, 90% of the elderly poor were receiving significant benefits through Social Security cost-of-living adjustments, through housing assistance, through Medicaid, and through other federal and state safeguards.

As a result of this triumph of social policy for senior citizens, many child advocates, including educators and politicians, insist that we can do the same for our most vulnerable citizens, our children. This persistent band is finally making progress toward changing the way society treats youngsters who are the innocent victims of accidents of birth or family misfortune.

But the scale of the problem is overwhelming. [Since 1975] . . . the incidence of poverty among children has increased and become complicated in ways that portend catastrophic consequences, not only for the children themselves, but also for our schools, our economy, and our social well-being.

Since 1975 children have been poorer than any other age group. By 1989 young people accounted for 39.5% of America's poor. The official U.S. poverty rate for all citizens in 1989 edged slightly downward to 13.1%—only a 2% decline from the Johnson era. Yet in raw numbers more Americans are poor today than before the War on Poverty. Nearly 40 million people of all ages live in families with income levels below the official poverty line of $7,704 for a family of two, $9,435 for a family of three, and $12,092 for a family of four. The current poverty rate is higher than during the worst recession years of the 1970s.

Actually, the real crisis for children and families is even worse than it first appears. Income for the average poor family in 1988 was $4,851 *below* the poverty line. For poor families headed by females, that gap was $5,206. Levels of family income this low mean that some serious family needs—such as food, clothing, medicine, early learning assistance, and housing—are not being met. The result for the children of these families is sickness, psychological stress, malnutrition, underdevelopment, and daily hardship that quickly takes its toll on their young minds and bodies.

Even though the postwar baby boom has long since subsided, nearly as many young people are poor today as when the War on Poverty was launched. However, the percentage today is higher. More than 12.6 million U.S. youngsters—nearly 20% of all children under the age of 18—are poor. Thus one in five American children goes to bed hungry or sick or cold.

And when these children wake each day, they face little prospect that the economic plight of their families will improve enough to make their lives better. Often they internalize the bleakness of their situation and blame themselves for it. Their lives become bitter and humorless or filled with anxiety and fear. Of course, many poor children retain their dignity, and their character is tempered by the Spartan battle for subsistence. But millions of others, permanently damaged, are unable to recover and fall victim to the vicious social pathology of poverty.

And the future seems even grimmer. [Former] U.S. Secretary of Education Lauro Cavazos has estimated that, by the year 2000, "as many as one-third of our young people will be disadvantaged and at risk."

Some American youngsters will never even have the chance to see the turn of the century. As has happened in other wars, they will perish. More than 10,000 children in the U.S. die each year as a direct result of the poverty they endure. Often they die during the first weeks of their lives because simple and inexpensive prenatal health care was unavailable to their mothers.

The U.S. has the highest rate of child poverty among the industrialized nations, nearly three times that of most other economically advanced nations. Moreover, the Children's Defense Fund, a leading Washington-based child advocacy group, has sadly noted that only the U.S. and South Africa, among the advanced industrial nations, do not provide universal health coverage for children and pregnant women and do not provide child care to foster early development.

The Younger, the Poorer

And the picture gets worse. The younger a child is in America today, the greater are his or her chances of being poor. According to the U.S. Census Bureau, the Americans most likely of all to be poor are those age 3 and under. Officially, 23.3% of this age group are poor. During the early years so critical to development, nearly one-fourth of U.S. children lack medical, nutritional, and early-learning assistance. Thus many poor children are needlessly condemned to physical and psychological deficiencies for the rest of their lives.

Further down the road, the social cost of this neglect will almost certainly be extravagant. Physical and mental damage that could have been prevented by inexpensive prenatal checkups or by nutritional programs in early childhood haunts our society in expensive educational, medical, welfare, and correctional costs that can reach into the hundreds of thousands of dollars. For example, 11% of children end up in special education classes because of cognitive and developmental problems, many of which could have been prevented by prenatal care. Even a pragmatist can count. The willful neglect of America's poor children is not only immoral; it is just plain stupid.

Children of poverty who make it through their earliest years relatively unscathed face new hardships later on. Nearly 22% of 3- to 5-year-olds are poor. Then, after six years of material want, most poor children enter school and make their first significant contact with a social institution. Indeed, the largest group of poor children ranges between the ages of 6 and 11. More than four million of these children—19.9% of the age group—continue to grow up in unremitting destitution.

Schools should be equipped to help these children gain skills to cope with and ultimately to escape from their economic circumstances. But far too many schools fail far too many poor children. And poor communities tend to get stuck with poor schools as patterns of taxation make a bad situation worse.

Only as children enter their teenage years—and begin to confront a new set of social and biological problems—does the poverty rate actually dip. But even among young people between the ages of 12 and 17, more than 16% live below the poverty line. That figure is higher than the poverty rate for the general population.

The Carnegie Council on Adolescent Development has emphasized that, between the ages of 10 and 15, young people are extremely volatile. For poor teens, the match is even closer to the fuse, since these youngsters are often besieged by problems of school failure, pregnancy, substance abuse, and economic stress.

These young people suffer not only the immediate physical and psychological damage of economic and social adversity; the long-term effects of their childhood deprivation and neglect also manifest themselves in a growing complex of social ills. One-

fourth of young black men are reported to have trouble of some
kind with correctional authorities. Illiteracy among poor dropouts is endemic. And the personal tragedy of broken homes and a
future of perpetually low-paying jobs feeds young black men into
the drug trade—and the morgue. The popular appeal of Jesse
Jackson's slogan, "Up with Hope," demonstrates just how many
young people are growing up in the hopelessness that poverty
breeds.

Young Families, Poor Children

Then there is the matter of family circumstances. Almost 50%
of all U.S. children living in a family headed by a person 25 years
of age or younger are poor. One-third of all children living in a
family headed by a person 30 years of age or younger are poor. In
fact, while the nation's overall poverty rate slowly declined from
1967 to 1987, the poverty rate for children living in a family
headed by a person 30 years of age or younger shot up from 19%
to 35.6%.

Likewise, if a child lives in a family headed by a woman, the
chances are better than 50/50 that the child is poor. More than
56% of families headed by single black women are poor. The
poverty rate for families headed by Hispanic women is 59%. Yet
single-parent families do not necessarily cause poverty. Half of
the nation's poor children live with both parents.

Contrary to popular perception, child poverty is not a phenomenon confined to the inner cities. Fewer than 9% of America's poor people live in the nation's core cities. The largest
number of poor people still live in semi-isolation in towns and
hamlets across the country. About 17% of these people are hidden in rural America. Just as in the inner cities, poverty rates in
some rural areas have reached 50% and higher. And some rural
regions have been poor for generations. Surprisingly, 28% of
America's poor struggle amidst the affluence of suburban communities, shut out from most of the benefits that their neighbors
enjoy. Westchester County, New York, one of the 11 wealthiest
suburban areas in the country, now has more than 5,000 homeless
people looking for shelter.

Another inaccurate perception about poverty is that being
poor is directly related to race. Two-thirds of poor Americans are
white. The Children's Defense Fund calculates that one white
child in seven is poor. However, the rate of poverty is consider-

ably higher for minorities, who are fast becoming majority demographic groups in the 10 largest states. Four out of nine black children are poor; three out of eight Hispanic children are poor. Poverty in America knows no racial boundaries, no geographic borders. The only common denominator for the children of poverty is that they are brought up under desperate conditions beyond their control—and, for them, the rhetoric of equal opportunity seems a cruel hoax, an impossible dream.

The Flip Side of Prosperity

During the "get-rich-quick" decade of the 1980s, when the number of U.S. billionaires quintupled, child poverty jumped by 23%. More than 2.1 million children tumbled into poverty as the stock market first soared, then plummeted, and finally rebounded. The bull market, with its leveraged buyouts, $325 billion savings-and-loan ripoffs, tax cuts for the wealthy, and junk bond scams, did little to drive up the value of children on the domestic agenda.

"The story of child poverty has become a story of American decline," a congressional staffer who works on poverty-related legislative issues recently lamented. "People have a vague sense that we are doing something wrong nationally, that we are going to be in trouble in the near future. The plight of children is related to this feeling. In addition to being immoral, our treatment of children is profoundly shortsighted. It is economically and socially shortsighted to allow children to grow up with unhealthy bodies and lousy educations and poor nutrition and inadequate health care. We all know that, but now it looks like it will kill us in the 21st century."

What makes matters worse is that the poor are getting poorer. According to the U.S. House of Representatives' Select Committee on Children, Youth, and Families, the income gap between families with the highest incomes and those with the lowest was wider in 1988 than in any year since 1947. The poorest 20% of families received less than 5% of the national income, while the wealthiest 20% received 44%, the largest share ever recorded. Maurice Zeitlin, a sociologist at the University of California, Los Angeles, recently concluded that the richest 1% of families own 42% of the net wealth of all U.S. families—a staggering proportion that has changed little since the 19th century. This super-rich elite owns 20% of all real estate, 60% of all corporate stock, and

80% of family-owned trusts. These huge disparities make the familiar excuses about budget deficits and tax burdens standing in the way of helping children seem feeble at best.

The vast and ongoing transformation of the U.S. economy from manufacturing to service jobs and from local to global markets has also harmed poor families. When the unemployment of the recession of the 1980s finally began to ease, many of the new jobs were service jobs that paid half as much as manufacturing jobs. According to Michael Sherraden, a professor at Washington University in St. Louis, "The overwhelming reality is that most new jobs being created today are very low-skilled service jobs with low pay and no benefits, not high-tech jobs."

Statistics from the U.S. Department of Labor show that, although the unemployment rate has fallen steadily since 1983, the poverty rate has remained high. Since 1983 unemployment has dropped by 4%. Meanwhile, the overall poverty rate has fallen only 2%—and has actually increased for children.

Working Harder, Getting Poorer

U.S. Census Bureau figures reveal that nearly half of the heads of all poor households are employed. In 1988 the proportion of poor heads of households who worked full-time increased by 1.8%. But that was accompanied by a decline in the average earnings of full-time male workers. A low minimum wage offers one explanation for this stubborn trend. For example, full-time work at the minimum wage by the head of a family of three leaves that family $2,500 below the poverty line.

In nearly 42% of poor households headed by females, the women are employed. About 10% work full-time, year-round. And 87% of poor children live in a family in which at least one person is employed at least part of the time. However, from 1979 to 1987 income for young families with children dropped by nearly 25%.

"The public has a misconception about who the poor are," Sherraden observes. "Most people who live below the poverty line are not welfare recipients and members of the underclass. They are people who have jobs or are members of a household in which someone has a job." He adds, "What kind of message are we delivering if people work hard and still do not make it?"

Some of the workers in poor families are children and teenagers. In 1989 the U.S. Department of Labor discovered 23,000 minors working in violation of the Fair Labor Standards Act. In fact, child labor violations have doubled in the last five years. Most such violations have involved young teenagers working too many hours or under unsafe conditions. Unlike the sweatshops of the past, many violators of child labor laws today are hamburger joints and fast-food establishments. Many teenagers work long hours because they must do so in order to survive, not because they are trying to buy designer jeans or are exploring future careers in food services. And, as teachers know, working often becomes a reason for classroom failure.

Cutbacks and Reductions

To add to an already bad situation, government cutbacks and the perpetual budget crisis have increased children's woes. The House Select Committee on Children, Youth, and Families found that, since 1970, the median grant through Aid to Families with Dependent Children (AFDC) has fallen 23%, from $471 to $361 in constant dollars. In 1987 AFDC reached only 56% of children in poverty, a lower proportion than in 1964 when the first volley was fired in the War on Poverty.

"Child poverty is Ronald Reagan's legacy to the 1990s," according to Rep. George Miller (D-Calif.), who chairs the Select Committee on Children, Youth, and Families. Between 1980 and 1988, during President Reagan's military build-up, the U.S. government spent $1.9 trillion on national defense, while cutting $10 billion from programs aimed at protecting poor children and families.

According to the Center for the Study of Social Policy, AFDC benefits and food stamps for a family of four amounted to only 66.3% of the 1988 poverty line, down from 70.9% in 1980. Meanwhile, participation in the food stamp program has declined 14% since 1982.

At the same time, federal assistance for low-income housing tumbled 76% when adjusted for inflation. In *The Same Client: The Demographics of Education and Service Delivery Systems,* a recent report from the Institute for Educational Leadership, the Institute for Educational Leadership, Harold Hodgkinson concluded that many dropouts and school failures can be attributed directly to such basic factors as the high cost of housing that eats up most of a family's available and limited income. Children living on the

edge of homelessness are prevented from finding the stability
that usually makes successful schooling possible.

"If low-income children were living in economically and socially secure housing with some rent protection, there is little
doubt that most of them could stay out of poverty and in school,
while their parents stay on the job and off welfare," Hodgkinson
advised in the report. He argued that national housing strategies
to increase the availability and reduce the cost of housing are
essential, if we wish to limit poverty. So are preventive social strategies that help people who are facing financial emergencies to
stay out of poverty.

No Place to Call Home

Poor housing or no housing—those seem to be the options
facing most poor children. Homeless children are one more dis-
tressing by-product of the new poverty that plagues this nation.
The U.S. Department of Education estimates that 220,000 school-
aged children are homeless and that 65,000 of them do not attend
school. About 15,600 homeless children live in publicly operated
shelters, 90,700 live in privately operated shelters, 55,750 stay
with relatives or friends, and 63,170 live "elsewhere." The greatest number of homeless children live in Los Angeles, New York,
Chicago, Minneapolis, and Houston. Homelessness among children in the nation's capital has increased by a factor of five in
recent years.

A report from the General Accounting Office estimated that,
on any given night, 186,000 children who are not actually homeless are "precariously housed," living on the verge of homelessness. The Department of Health and Human Services calculates that, over the course of a year, as many as one million
youngsters under age 18 lack a permanent home or live on the
streets.

Despite the $1.7 billion in federal funds expended through
the Stewart B. McKinney Homeless Assistance Act of 1987 and
the millions more spent through the Runaway and Homeless
Youth Act of 1974, homelessness continues to grow—a disturbing
reminder that not all is well in the land of the free.

The future also looks bleak for those categories of young
people who no longer live at home, according to the House Select
Committee on Children, Youth, and Families. Its late 1989 report,

No Place to Call Home: Discarded Children in America, concluded that by 1995 nearly a million children no longer living with their parents will cause serious problems for the schools. The study found that between 1985 and 1988 the number of children living in foster care jumped by 23%, while federal funding for welfare services for children rose only 7%.

Foster children are only one of the categories of displaced children, most of whom come from poor families. The number of children in juvenile detention centers rose 27% between 1979 and 1987, while funding fell from $100 million to $66.7 million. The number of children in mental health facilities also soared by 60% between 1983 and 1986. Meanwhile, federal block grants for mental health services declined by $17 million.

Drug and alcohol abuse by parents contributed to these dangerous trends. From 1985 to 1988 the number of children born with drug exposure quadrupled, reaching 375,000 in 1988. Add to that the number of abused or neglected children, which climbed 82% between 1981 and 1988. Of course, not all of these children are poor, but needy children fall into these categories much more frequently than their not-needy counterparts.

Rep. Miller warned that the nation's schools could be "overwhelmed" by such problems in the 1990s. He noted that teachers, counselors, and social workers are already overworked and that none of them "receives the training needed to deal with the complex and difficult problems confronting children and families today."

Clearly, no social problem operates in isolation. Poverty breeds personal and social disintegration. Difficulties in the areas of health, housing, and education are all linked. For example, significant numbers of homeless children suffer a wide range of health disorders. Many risk hearing loss because of untreated ear infections. That in turn leads to serious learning problems. In many homeless shelters, such infectious diseases as tuberculosis and whooping cough run rampant among uninoculated youngsters. Poverty is more than a social label; it is a disease that weakens and often destroys its victims.

Healthy Goals, Unhealthy Results

At first glance, it seems that the U.S. has a comprehensive health-care system. For example, we spent $551 billion on health care in 1987. But 37 million Americans, including more than 12 million children, have no health insurance. Uninsured children have a 20% greater chance of poor health and are less likely to have proper immunization against infectious diseases.

Nearly half of all poor children do not receive benefits from Medicaid, despite recent congressional action ordering states to provide more extensive coverage to poor children and pregnant mothers. The National Commission to Prevent Infant Mortality has found that the U.S. ranks 20th among the nations of the world in infant mortality and has urged Congress to take over Medicaid to insure that it reaches *all* infants and pregnant mothers.

This year the Pepper Commission, a bipartisan group of congressional representatives, urged a massive overhaul of the national health system, which is "in total crisis." Among other reforms, the commission called for universal protection for poor children and families. But the $66 billion a year price tag has scared off many potential supporters.

One pregnant woman in four receives no prenatal care during the critical first trimester. Such a mother is three to six times more likely to give birth to a premature, low-birth-weight baby who will be at risk for developmental disability or even death. Ultimately, 10.6 of every 1,000 newborns in the U.S. die—the highest rate in the developed world.

In 1980 Dr. Julius Richmond, then surgeon general of the U.S., published a list of 20 health-care goals for infants and children to be achieved by 1990. Like the recent list of educational goals promulgated by President Bush and the National Governors' Association, the health-care targets were ambitious and essential to heading off social and economic crisis. But by late 1989 the American Academy of Pediatrics, an organization of 37,000 experts on children's medical health, concluded that only one of the 20 goals had been achieved.

That one success was in reducing neonatal mortality: the death rate for infants in the first 28 days after birth has dropped from 9.5 to 6.4 deaths per 1,000. However, other goals, such as improving birth weights and prenatal care and narrowing the gap between racial groups in infant mortality, remain unfulfilled. The mortality rate for black infants is still twice that for white infants, about the same as it was 26 years ago; the infant mortality rate for the entire U.S. population stands at 10.1%, while the rate for African-Americans is 17.9%. (By contrast, the infant mortality rate in Japan is just 4.8%.) Moreover, surviving black infants have nine times more chance than white infants of being neurologically impaired.

Dr. Myron Wegman of the University of Michigan School of Public Health, who conducted the study for the pediatricians, discovered the existence of two separate medical nations within this land. One nation is prosperous, with the latest in health technology and knowledge at its disposal; the other nation is deprived, with death rates and health problems that match those commonly found in the Third World. Dr. Wegman blamed government cuts in health programs and social services during the Reagan Administration for a slowdown that prevented reaching the goals.

Impact on Schools

What do the mountains of statistics and a heritage of damaged lives mean for educators in the public schools? Surveys of teachers have found disturbing news. The Metropolitan Life Insurance Company's annual *Survey of the American Teacher* discovered that in 1989 American teachers were greatly alarmed at the health and social problems of their students.

Other surveys show that teachers worry about constant pupil turnover, about students' health problems, and about students' preoccupation with family problems. Once again, such concerns are more common among teachers of children from low-income families. Guidance counselors report that, even at the elementary level, they find themselves "dealing with one crisis after another" in a child's life.

Teachers also report that they are seeing more children with learning disabilities. In fact, over the last 10 years the number of children diagnosed as learning disabled has increased 140%—to about 1.9 million children. While educators argue over the meaning of the term and debate possible reasons for the increase, veteran teachers claim that they have never before seen so many children with problems of comprehension and basic skills in their classes.

According to Verna Gray, a veteran teacher in the Chicago schools, poverty leads to more problems than just the lack of the basic academic skills needed to succeed in school. "Many of these youngsters don't have any self-esteem or even the belief that they can achieve," she notes.

The effects on the schools of increasing numbers of children living in poverty may not be completely clear, and the details are certainly debatable. But no one disputes that there are serious effects—or that the effects are negative. . . . [The final part of this article appears in Section Four of this compilation.]

III. HOW WE GOT HERE: CAUSES OF HOMELESSNESS

EDITOR'S INTRODUCTION

Throughout the articles presented thus far in this compilation, mention has been made of the sources of homelessness—housing shortages, mental illness, substance addiction, the economy, and the lethal combination of childhood and poverty. This section examines causes not already addressed elsewhere in this book.

Within the general public, and perhaps among some less informed members of its wealthy and political elite, there are two groups stereotypically expected to be among the homeless—the mentally ill and the substance-addicted. The first two articles in this section examine the appearance of these groups among the homeless and account for their presence in today's homeless population. According to the variety of statistics already presented in prior articles, each of these two segments account for between one quarter and one third of all the homeless in America today, and an arguably larger proportion of the terminally versus the temporarily displaced.

In a book review reprinted from *Commentary* Dr. Joseph Adelson, a professor of psychology, discusses the origins of the homeless mentally ill. Addressing both philosophical points of view within the mental health profession as well as political pressures to release mental patients from traditional institutional settings, Dr. Adelson concludes that the system which put the mentally infirm on the streets without the facilities to support them was both overambitious and ill-conceived and caused "perhaps the greatest social-policy fiasco of an era which specialized in them." At the root of this is what the author labels a radically egalitarian anti-psychiatry movement.

Next, David Whitman, Dorian Friedman, and Laura Thomas, writing in *U.S. News & World Report,* examine the return of skid row. The authors point out that the media view of the homeless focuses on families primarily and thereby distort the reality of who is on the street. Chronic alcoholics and drug abusers, they claim, are a fast growing segment of homeless America, more prevalent now than in the 1950s and 1960s when the image of skid-row homelessness was predominant. Factors contributing to the return of skid row include the disappearance of traditional flophouses to make way for gentrification and downtown development, looser regulation of drunkenness and substance abuse by law enforcement agencies, and the advent of crack cocaine. Aggravating the problem is the dearth of programs to help addicts kick their habits. Meanwhile, public sympathy is in as short supply as government sources of funding to deal with the new residents of skid row.

Writing from a different perspective, C. C. Bruno in an article reprinted from *The Humanist* tells of his own experiences as part of the legion of homeless and the variety of social factors he believes contributed to the situation in which he found himself. Among these are the influx of illegal alien agricultural workers, lack of housing, unrealistic minimum wage requirements, and government bureaucracy and policy mismanagement. Perhaps most important in perpetuating the problem is the government and public's myopic view of who the homeless are and what their needs are.

Perhaps the most insidious aspect of the homeless problem is the type of quick-fix solutions being used by many local and city governments. James N. Baker highlights some of these in an article from *Newsweek*. Intolerance and frustration rather than genuine sympathy and the desire to help have all too often marked public policy in our cities. Genuine efforts at reform are replaced by steps that merely move the homeless out of sight. The result is the perpetuation of rather than solution to the problem.

THE IDEOLOGY OF HOMELESSNESS[1]

Every once in a while a deranged man appears across the street from my office, shouting loudly but incoherently about a conspiracy threatening him. After several hours he disappears;

[1]Article by Joseph Adelson, professor of psychology at the University of Michigan, from *Commentary* 91:32+ Mr '91. Copyright © 1991 by the American Jewish Committee. Reprinted with permission.

presumably someone comes to take him away. But then he reappears in a few weeks, or a few months, and the scene is repeated. I once mentioned him to a colleague, also a psychotherapist, who said I ought to count my blessings since he shows up only so often. My colleague's office is located not too far from a halfway house, and on the streets near his building there are so many strange and disorderly people that some of his patients are fearful and want him to move. He does not blame them, he is sometimes frightened himself. He shakes his head sadly and asks: "How in the world did we ever get into this mess?"

The short, flip answer to his question is that we took a large but manageable problem—caring for the long-term mentally ill—put our Best Minds to work on it, and produced a vast and unmanageable problem, the psychotic homeless. The somewhat longer answer runs along these lines: the traditional mental hospital was disliked by almost everyone. It was costly, it was ineffective, much of the time it served only as a warehouse, and some of the time it was the snakepit so vividly depicted in film, fiction, and exposé journalism. It survived only because there seemed no other option. Then, unexpectedly, an alternative appeared, one produced by apparent progress on two fronts: the emergence of anti-psychotic medication and the development of new ideas about psychosis itself, to the effect that mental illness was rooted in and sustained by malevolent environments, one of which was the mental hospital. By emptying such institutions, not only would the state save untold sums of money, but the patients locked up inside would be liberated, would lead far better lives outside, and might even be cured of what were possibly pseudo-illnesses.

The hospitals were emptied, and disaster followed—it was perhaps the greatest social-policy fiasco of an era which specialized in them. Nothing worked as it was supposed to do. The medications were helpful, but they were not the panaceas advertised. They were not always effective, they sometimes produced serious side effects, many patients refused or could not remember to take them. The substitutes for the hospitals—community centers of various kinds—were not in fact established, or were given over to activities interesting mostly to the mental-health profession, such as providing outpatient psychotherapy for the not-so-disturbed. Then, when one counted the indirect costs of alternate care, or of no care at all, it became evident that there were no financial savings to be had. By the time all these problems were recognized, there were tens of thousands of insane people on the streets, most of them helpless and vulnerable, some dangerous to themselves and others.

The conventional assessment of what went wrong agrees that serious mistakes were made, that we were overly optimistic about what we could accomplish. But as this school of thought sees it, our errors grew out of enthusiasm, out of that activist ardor, characteristically American, which is ever ready to innovate and try out the untried. In this case the experiment failed, but we learned some valuable lessons and will do better next time. Back to the drawing board.

The account seems plausible but is in fact seriously misleading. The decision to empty the mental hospitals was not simply a mistaken judgment. It was an ideological decision deriving from strong convictions about both the nature of psychosis and the function of the hospital. These in turn reflected powerful though often unvoiced assumptions about human nature and the social order. If we had not made those assumptions we would not have made the errors we did. There is, in short, a connection leading from some of the books in my office—books on political philosophy and academic psychology—and that tortured man across the street, wandering up and down the sidewalk and shouting at the heavens.

To trace that connection we could begin from any number of starting points, but a good one might be American academic psychology in the 1950's, then all but dominated by behaviorist learning theory. The true psychological scientist, according to the behaviorists, must concentrate on what was visible and external and measurable, and eschew speculating about such ineffables as "the mind." The mind was merely a hypothesis, and even if there were such an entity it could be reached only by the slow, steady building of models based on stimulus and response. All else was woolgathering.

These ideas, as Gordon Allport of Harvard, a (quiet) opponent of behaviorism, wrote in the mid-1950's, had their origins in the empiricist tradition deriving from John Locke. As Allport characterized that position, since "mind is by nature a *tabula rasa,* it is not the organism but what happens to the organism from outside that is important." And indeed in its earliest, purest version, behaviorism was the heir not only of Locke but of the Enlightenment more generally. In the work of the American psychologist J. B. Watson (1878–1958), behaviorism revived the Enlightenment formula for human perfectibility by rejecting the importance of innate differences and by promoting (in the words of John Passmore) "the conviction that men can be improved to an unlimited degree by controlling the formation of their habits." These were not merely hypothetical possibilities for Watson. One of his major works, *Behaviorism,* was a remarkably self-confident statement of the nearly infinite capacity of behavioral techniques to produce what we want in human conduct.

One might imagine that the Lockean tradition has by now been routed. Who still believes in an organism empty, passive, entirely pliable, lacking in will or purpose and without tendency? Even at the time Allport wrote, about thirty-five years ago, behaviorism was already losing its luster, and was being replaced by the cognitive approaches it once scornfully dismissed. Thus, the dominant voice in developmental psychology in those days was Jean Piaget, who posited complex intrinsic patterns of thinking which unfolded as the child grew. In addition, psychoanalytic psychologies were for the first time becoming respectable in the graduate departments, and that extraordinarily "full" system of internal tendencies was taken very seriously indeed. Even the most formidable contemporary behaviorist, B. F. Skinner, was beginning to seem quaint, his contribution now seen as merely providing a bag of tricks with which behavioral therapists discouraged bad habits.

Yet the Lockean tradition did not wither away. As with other strong ideas—true and false alike—it managed to survive and prosper, doing so by assuming a new identity. Like a revenant, the Lockean spirit departed one host and attached itself to a more receptive one, in this case moving from the learning laboratory to social theories of human conduct, now become aggressively political.

The strategy was to devalue the concept of personality, by denying, first, that it is consistent over time and, second, that it is an important determinant of behavior. Personality was said to be something of a chimera—there is less there than meets the eye. We imagine a degree of consistency we cannot really demonstrate. People will be selfish one moment, altruistic the next. Children who will not cheat in one situation will do so in another—indeed, there are strong findings to this effect, or so it was said. Why should we believe in the existence of traits like honesty or altruism, given how hard it is to nail down their presence?

If such qualities are illusory or ephemeral, and do not govern conduct, then what does? The answer was "the situation," the influence of the immediate milieu, its expectations and constraints: I am "honest" not because of a deeply entrenched character trait, let alone the promptings of the superego, but because I fear the consequences of being caught. If I see others cheating or stealing, and if it is clear I will not be found out, I will not be "honest." *Autres temps, autres moeurs,* even over the short run. People are neither good nor evil, they are reflections of the milieu, and much of the time of their immediate surroundings.

So said, and says, situationism, which I have put here in its purest form, absent the usual qualifications and escape hatches. Like behaviorism, it too is by no means a new idea. It can be traced back to the sociologist W. I. Thomas, in an important essay appearing in the 1920's. Gardner Murphy's influential textbook on personality, published in 1947, gave a full chapter to situationism. But in Murphy's version the situation is only one of a large number of variables influencing conduct, most of which are such factors as traits, needs, defenses, and emotions. In the 1960's and 70's a new and tougher version set itself to expunge those variables, to demonstrate the hegemony of situation *per se*. In the most famous situational experiments, the studies of obedience conducted by Stanley Milgram, an unsuspecting person is persuaded by the "experimenter" to administer ostensibly dangerous electric shocks to ostensible research subjects. In another well-known example, ordinary undergraduates are induced to play the role of prison guards and soon enough lose themselves in beastliness. These demonstrations are quite compelling, seeming to prove that ordinary people can be coerced by "situation" so as to behave in absurd or aberrant or even abhorrent ways.

Yet if one looks at the studies closely, some troubling questions arise. Do they in fact simulate the "reality" they set out to duplicate, and do the "laws" discovered travel beyond the demonstration? Even if they do, they tell us only about short-term events, as though life were composed only of vignettes. What would a longer perspective tell us about the human career? Above all, the demonstrations prove compelling only at first blush; once variations are introduced on the original experiments, so many exceptions and ambiguities emerge as to make us wonder whether we have discovered anything that says much or means much.

These logical and empirical problems, serious enough on their own, are overshadowed by an avalanche of findings which contradict the major tenets of situationism (in its strong version). We now know with some certainty that personality is remarkably consistent over time. A personality test taken in one's teens will yield essentially the same results when taken again in one's fifties. Ratings of a person made early in life by others even correlate highly with such ratings in adulthood. The most impressive findings of all are those demonstrating the long-term effects of personality; thus, children rated as undercontrolled in childhood (ages eight to ten) are more likely to be downwardly mobile, or those rated as shy lag behind their peers in such matters as getting married. Even more startling is the evidence from various studies which show a relationship between early mortality and subtle measures of personal style in early adulthood.

The wonder is that situationism was taken seriously in the first place. Anyone who has raised children will attest both to the consistency of character and to its effect on how lives are lived. The reclusive, pensive child will likely remain that way, and will likely lead a different life from that of his gregarious brother. Anyone who has lived long enough will observe the same consistency in his friends. A boy I knew in high school is now an economic analyst who appears frequently on television, and watching him I am transfixed by how little he has changed: the same body language, facial expressions, intonations of voice, above all the same mocking wit, once directed at the fools who taught us, now deployed against the fools who make our economic policy. Of course these are merely anecdotes and not systematic findings, let alone scientific proof. But there has always been enough empirical information to rebut the assumptions of situationism, as in the revealing studies by the Gluecks and by Lee Robins showing close connections between certain forms of childhood disorder and criminality later in life.

Something, however, was in the air when situationism was introduced—something political—and we get a glimpse of it if we return to Gardner Murphy's treatment of 1947. Well before the civil-rights movement or the onset of feminism, Murphy wanted to show that traits imputed to blacks or Jews or Italians or women are responses to the situations they find themselves in. Psychology, he wrote, demonstrates that "there are no large and socially important differences . . . based on racial stock," and the traits said to characterize a member of a given group—desirable and undesirable alike—are best understood "as reflections of the situation in which he is placed and of the roles which he must enact."

Yet even so, Murphy did not go so far as to assume that

circumstance and role were the *sole* answer to behavior; cultural and other differences could be real and perdurable. It was this latter conclusion that was swept away when an egalitarian zeal overtook the social sciences. All differences were not suspect, and many were anathema. Everyone, it was now asserted, is equal: if some score differently on tests, something is wrong with the measure, or how the measure is taken, or it is the result of how we have been raised, or the expectations we have internalized, or the signals given off by those teaching us or testing us. The differences that are undeniably there have been produced by upbringing alone, and are neither biological nor constitutional nor hereditary in origin.

Aaron Wildavsky of Berkeley has termed this state of mind "radical egalitarianism," and in a series of penetrating essays has demonstrated its spread throughout the elite culture. According to its tenets, all differences reflecting "hierarchy" are inherently suspect and reprehensible—men over women, white over black, rich over poor. The new egalitarian passion reaches out, in fact, to *all* relations marked by unequal status—Third World vs. First World, mature vs. young (children's rights), humans against other species (animal rights). Perhaps its most unexpected extension has been to behavior once considered not merely different but socially or morally deviant—homosexuality is the most striking example here, but also drug abuse and to a lesser extent criminality.

We can see how comfortably psychosis fits into the Lockean formula and its egalitarian extension. The notion that personality is insubstantial, transient, illusory, had its counterpart in a new understanding of psychosis—that it too is not a fixed condition but is fluid and changes with the moment; indeed, that it might not be present at all, but only an illusion. In this understanding, "craziness" is a term we use to shut away people who are merely different, independent, or eccentric. They listen to a different drummer. What we term insanity is often no more than a heightened sensitivity to the craziness of the world, or to the truly mad behavior of the so-called normals. Some psychotics are visionaries, seeing truths the rest of us can reach only through mind-altering drugs. And since psychosis is not biological, not fixed, and not intractable, it should not be "treated" unless the person affected so wishes.

The attack on the idea of psychosis might have remained largely academic—that is, without practical effect—were it not coupled with an equally vigorous attack on the mental hospital. The underlying purpose of the hospital, it was now said, is to imprison those we find deviant, hence offensive. It is an instrument of social control, a way the state has developed to remove certain types of troublemakers, especially those who are not clearly "criminal," but merely burdensome or troubling. In any case, the hospital cannot cure its occupants, since they do not suffer from disease. To the contrary, the hospital intensifies the condition by confirming the label of "crazy" which the community has already affixed. In this way the hospital helps to create the very condition it is supposed to treat: the hospital "situation" induces "insanity" much as Milgram's experiments produced "cruelty."

The problem, in short, is not in the person but in the milieu: over the years, this view was set forth by several writers, most brilliantly by the sociologist Erving Goffman, whose métier was a crystalline depiction of environments. He surpassed himself in the book *Asylums,* written from the inside (as a pretended staff member) and capturing the claustral surrealism of the mental hospital. But however compelling it was, *Asylums* was still reportage. What was needed was something "empirical," hence scientifically respectable. Some years later that and more was to be provided when the prestigious journal *Science* published an article by Stanford's David Rosenhan that was to have a profound effect on both the idea of psychosis and our view of the hospital.

Rosenhan inserted normal people into mental hospitals to see if they would be detected. The pseudo-patients were instructed to report schizophrenic symptoms in order to gain admission but to behave normally thereafter. They were not found out. The staff regarded them as genuine psychotics. The demonstration was taken as proof that sane and insane are not sharply demarcated categories, and inferentially that the hospitals are filled with mildly disturbed or even normal people who are locked up for no good reason. Rosenhan's article was a smashing success, becoming the most widely cited and reprinted article in psychology, the crowning empirical achievement of the movement against psychiatry.

In the fullness of time we are able to see that the Rosenhan demonstration is itself illusory. It demonstrates only that hospitals, like other bureaucratic institutions, tend to take the given for granted and to follow routine. It also shows, what did not need to be shown, that it is easy to carry out an imposture, especially when there is no reason to suspect one. The Rosenhan study now seems badly outdated, and the same may be said for anti-psychiatry as a whole, which lingers on only among the hopelessly ideologized. The question to ask, as with situationism, is why it was believed in the first place. For it too violates ordinary experience.

To be sure, not all psychotics are psychotic all of the time. There are ups and downs, there are long periods of remission, there are many cases where insanity is a once-in-a-lifetime event. But that does not disprove the fact that psychosis exists or that those suffering from it are unable to care for themselves. The first such person I ever saw was a fifteen-year-old boy who carried on a combative conversation with an invisible person located behind me. The most recent was a hospitalized woman who believed that her six-year-old daughter was in league with the devil, and must be put to death. These are by no means unusual examples. How can we imagine them to be nothing more than eccentricities or modest variations of normality? How can we expect such persons to assume full responsibility for themselves? And how in the world could we ignore so blithely powerful evidence—not nearly as overwhelming as it later became, but of sufficient weight to have given us pause—that biological factors play a significant role in the genesis of psychosis? Why did anti-psychiatry mesmerize, and for so long a time?

Many of the answers can be found in a dazzling new book on mental illness, *Madness in the Streets*, by Rael Jean Isaac and Virginia Armat. One of several full-scale treatments of the problem to appear in the last few years, it is to my mind the best, an intellectual as well as a social and political history. Isaac and Armat spell out the ways in which the doctrines of anti-psychiatry weakened our sense of obligation to a group, many of whom are genuinely helpless, by claiming that they were not psychotic at all but only the victims of poverty and racism, or prisoners of a callous government. The complex realities of diagnosis, cure, and treatment were thereby reduced to the level of Ken Kesey's famous novel *One Few Over the Cuckoo's Nest*, with its melodramatic portrait of innocents wrongly accused, helpless in the hands of cruel pseudo-healers.

Isaac and Armat's presentation is not either/or; it recognizes at every moment that methods of diagnosis and treatment have themselves been abused or used recklessly and that they do not

always provide cures, let alone miraculous ones. But the politiciz-
ing of mental illness, in the belief that it is one more example of
the powerful oppressing the weak, has led to a bizarre state of
affairs where those who would certainly be helped, and might
indeed be cured, are kept from appropriate therapies. Anyone
still believing that, in the disciplines of psychiatry and psychology,
science easily overcomes dogma should read the section of this
book entitled "The War Against Treatment," in which the authors
show how weak, irrelevant, or nonexistent findings were all allowed to trash good research in forums responsible for making
public policy.

Reading these accounts one is reminded again of the remarkable power of the judiciary in setting policy, often to disastrous
effect. The "right to refuse treatment," noble as it may sound in
principle, has had nothing but wretched consequences for psychotics, for their families, and for the community at large. A
practitioner in the field hears about such cases constantly—the
"Billie Boggs" case in New York is merely the most notorious—in
which a person clearly out of control but refusing care is bounced
from the police to the emergency room to the hospital to the
family and ultimately to the streets. One might excuse the judges,
on the grounds that they know not what they do. It is hard to be
quite so forgiving of my own profession, which helped establish
these policies and continues to aid and abet them even after their
bankruptcy has become fully evident.

Isaac and Armat discuss an important California case, involving the right to refuse medication, in which *amicus* briefs were
filed by both the American Orthopsychiatric and American Psychological Associations, the former using "wildly exaggerated figures, not backed up by research," the latter offering arguments
that Isaac and Armat correctly term "extraordinary," among them
the idea that delusion and hallucination are rights protected by
the First Amendment. On the question of whether medication
may be helpful in calming violently agitated patients, the brief
recommends instead such techniques as seclusion, strait-jackets,
and cold wet-packs—in short, all of the methods used in the
snakepit asylum which led to the attack on the mental hospital in
the first place.

Anti-psychiatry will sooner or later vanish, its demise aided by
this devastating book. But the longer, deeper tradition that produced and sustains it simply carries on, telling us that nothing of

real importance can be found within the skin, that it is all out there. The last national convention of the American Psychological Association presented a two-day mini-convention on homelessness which paraded all the standard errors. Speaker after speaker—psychologists and psychiatrists all—argued against too much attention being given to the psychological. One of them inveighed against funding research into substance use and mental illness as contributors to the plight of the homeless. What then is responsible? Why, our old friends poverty and racism. And what is to be done? Why, call in some other old friends, "empowerment" and "action research" and "innovative interventions," along with such new ones as "ecological resource perspectives."

Empty organism, empty diagnosis, empty solutions. And in the meantime, that deranged man across the street from my office goes on shaking the heavens—and everyone around him—with his tormented cries.

THE RETURN OF SKID ROW[2]

The images are poignant, if misleading. In recent weeks, a CBS docudrama depicted the woes of a white working-class couple forced to move to a shelter after their apartment burned down. Jesse Jackson deplored the fact that families with children are "the fastest-growing sector" of the homeless population. And the *Los Angeles Times* found a family that became homeless on Christmas Eve after a distraught neighbor mistakenly threw a Molotov cocktail through its bedroom window. (The neighbor was aiming at someone else's window.)

Yet such tales by the news media and homeless advocates of a "new" homeless population–families victimized by acts of God, economic misfortune and tight housing markets—convey only a partial picture of the changing homeless population. The sad truth is that the personal disabilities of today's homeless, particu-

[2]Article by David Whitman with Dorian Friedman and Laura Thomas, from *U.S. News & World Report* 108:27+ Ja 15 '90. Copyright Jan. 15, 1990 U.S. News & World Report. Reprinted with permission.

larly among single adults, strongly resemble those of the old skid-row homeless. In fact, chronic alcoholics and drug abusers are now the fastest-growing group among those living in the streets and shelters, so much so that substance abuse is slightly *more* prevalent among the new homeless than among their predecessors of the 1950s and 1960s, when the skid-row image of the homeless was predominant.

The growth in the population of homeless substance abusers stems from several factors, including the disappearance of the flophouse, looser regulation of public drunkenness and the advent of crack cocaine. And the increase in their number has exponentially swelled taxpayer payments for the homeless because their problems are far more intractable than those of the displaced families featured in most media accounts. Unfortunately, few soup kitchens and shelters do anything to help homeless substance abusers break their addiction. "To date," says Anna Kondratas, who oversees homeless-aid programs for the Department of Housing and Urban Development, "alcoholics and drug abusers have been pretty well ignored."

Although the extent of alcohol and drug abuse among the homeless varies considerably from city to city, national figures indicate that substance abuse now outstrips mental illness as the most serious health problem plaguing the urban homeless. A 27-city survey released last month by the U.S. Conference of Mayors found that local officials now estimate that 44 percent of the homeless are substance abusers (while about 25 percent are mentally ill). The survey also concluded that since 1986 the numbers of alcoholics and drug addicts have grown faster than other segments of the homeless, with their ranks increasing by almost a third in the last year alone. Even today, the bulk of homeless substance abusers are inebriates. A health project funded by the Robert Wood Johnson Foundation that treated some 83,000 homeless adults in 19 cities between 1985 and 1988 found 38 percent were chronic alcoholics and 13 percent were drug abusers. By contrast, extensive surveys of skid-row residents in the late 1950s and early 1960s concluded that only a fifth to a third of the homeless were alcoholics.

The Fading Flophouse

Despite the recent surge in substance abuse, alcohol and drug addiction among the homeless went largely unnoticed over the last decade—in part, ironically, because skid-row neighborhoods shrank. Prior to the 1980s, homeless alcoholics tended to be especially visible because they were concentrated in skid-row areas marked by cheap bars, flophouses and missions. During the 1970s, however, thousands of low-rent apartments in single-room-occupancy hotels (SRO's) on skid rows were razed or gentrified to make way for urban renewal, and homeless alcoholics became far more dispersed. In Los Angeles alone, more than half of the SRO units in the downtown area were demolished between 1970 and 1985. In New York's Bowery—an area once included in bus tours of Manhattan so guides could point out "scenes of depravity"—only one SRO hotel remained by 1987.

Besides the flophouse, the other traditional resting place for homeless drunks has been the jail cell. But during the 1970s, most states decriminalized public drunkenness, pushing inebriates out of jails and into the streets. Today, vagrancy, public drunkenness and disorderly conduct account for fewer than 12 percent of all arrests, compared with about 40 percent 20 years ago.

More recently, the advent of crack, a relatively cheap alternative to alcohol, has accelerated the epidemic of substance abuse among the homeless, especially among younger black and Hispanic men. In Philadelphia over the last two decades, the Diagnostic and Rehabilitation Center (DRC) detoxified tens of thousands of homeless adults, the vast majority of whom, up until 1987, were alcoholics. Now, however, more than half of the DRC's homeless clients have a primary diagnosis of crack addiction, and some 90 percent of the crack addicts are problem drinkers, too. In Washington, D.C., a random sampling of more than 400 shelter residents by Howard University psychologist Norweeta Milburn found about 15 percent had used crack within the previous month. And in Alameda County, Calif., the nonprofit Shelter Against Violent Environments, Inc. (SAVE), has even opened a transitional apartment complex just for homeless, battered women who are hooked on crack, alcohol and other drugs.

Stole Dad's Booze Money

Like the skid-row drunks of yesteryear, homeless crack users strain and often sever their ties with family, friends and the working world. Tina Baxter-Hill entered the SAVE transitional house with her 1-year-old daughter after getting hooked on crack, marijuana and alcohol. The 24-year-old recalls that after her crack highs she felt a "terrible depression—like I had lost a loved one." To obtain more crack, she started pawning her jewelry and clothes. When her hard-drinking father gave her $100 to hold for him because he was afraid he would spend it on booze, she rushed out and spent it on crack. Subsequently, she tried to commit suicide by taking an overdose of codeine pills—but then changed her mind in time to have her stomach pumped at the county hospital. Not until her boyfriend frightened her one day did Baxter-Hill take her daughter and move to the SAVE shelter. At SAVE, she participates in Narcotics Anonymous meetings and parental-stress groups, while her daughter attends day care.

Although Baxter-Hill has been drug-free for eight months now, the current shelter and social-service system generally does little to help the homeless battle their addictions and, in some instances, may actually impede recovery. By almost any standard, homeless substance abusers are extremely needy. They are more likely than the nonalcoholic homeless to remain on the streets for long periods of time, to have arrest records, to be alienated from friends and family, to be seriously ill and to be victims of street crime themselves. Yet according to a recent HUD survey two thirds of the nation's urban shelters provide no substance-abuse services. Many emergency shelters also refuse to admit heavy drinkers or drug addicts because they are disruptive.

To date, the federal government has earmarked $16.5 million in a nine-city demonstration program for homeless substance abusers, an amount that will provide an intensive level of treatment for just 3,300 individuals nationwide per year. In his recent housing package, President Bush did propose that $728 million in matching funds be provided to states and localities over a three-year period so federal housing assistance could be paired with more social services for homeless substance abusers and the mentally ill. So far, though, his plan has received a mixed reception in Congress.

For homeless substance abusers fortunate enough to receive treatment, a few days of detoxification is the norm. Unfortunately, about 3 out of 4 also leave detox without any referral for aftercare, and once they return to the streets, the shelters and the bottle gangs, it is not long before they are again hooked. Typically,

a homeless alcoholic goes through detox dozens of times, sometimes just to have a place to stay. One 39-year-old alcoholic interviewed for the Robert Wood Johnson health-care study confessed
to having been through detoxification 480 times.

Two Cases a Night

Several model programs have tried, with some success, to slow
the detox revolving door by offering intensive counseling and
transitional housing. In San Diego and Pittsburgh, municipal and
private groups have launched programs to rebuild SRO's. In
some cases, alcohol-free interim housing and the support of other
recovering addicts have helped even the most hard-core alcoholics. Bob Carothers, 59, recalls that he was drunk for "30 years
straight. I could drink two cases of beer a night—that was nothing." When he abandoned his second wife and two young children 18 years ago, he started living in the streets of Philadelphia.
Sometimes he slept in a '38 Buick that was up on blocks, sometimes on a park bench. Occasionally, he held odd jobs, but often
he would go for days without eating, just guzzling beer. "When
you did eat," Carothers explains, "you'd heave it up afterward
because your belly shrinks."

[In the summer of 1989,] fearful he would not last another
winter, Carothers finally entered a DRC detox program. [Since
then,] . . . he has lived at the DRC-run Washington House, a bar-
racks-style home that houses 35 men for anywhere from four to
six months while they recover from their alcohol or drug addiction. The recovery home requires Carothers and other men to
start resuming obligations; there are mandatory Breathalyzer
tests, for instance, and each tenant pays $120 a month in rent,
either from his job or welfare check. But unlike most shelters,
Washington House also provides rehabilitative services. Alcoholics Anonymous and Narcotics Anonymous groups and job
counseling are available on-site or at the DRC's main detox facility
so the men do not have to travel all over town for outpatient care.
"What we want to create," says DRC President Irving Shandler, "is
a sense of belonging."

At the house, onetime hardened drinkers and drug abusers
can be seen applauding each other for "sobriety anniversaries."
And that sense of shared enterprise, Carothers says, helps him
remain sober. In December [1989], he began working the night
shift as a maintenance man at a local hospital. [H]e even had a

reunion at a Dunkin' Donuts shop with his 21-year-old daughter—whom he had lost touch with for 18 years. "The whole time we were sitting there," he sighs, "she just held my hand and wouldn't let go."

Such model initiatives will probably remain a rarity, however. Dating back to the Okies of the 1930s, homeless families have long aroused public sympathy, while homeless "bums" have just as regularly provoked public derision. The tendency to dismiss homeless substance abusers seems pervasive in the media, too. A . . . study by the Center for Media and Public Affairs of 129 stories run by the three major networks and newsmagazines between November, 1986, and February, 1989, found that only 7 percent of the homeless portrayed in the accounts were drug or alcohol users. Robert Hayes, founder of the National Coalition for the Homeless, says he has fielded numerous calls from television producers who want him to find a white homeless family in New York City for an interview. When Hayes informed the producers that 90 percent of homeless families there are minorities, the producers inevitably responded: "We want a family that everyone can identify with." "Nine times out of 10," Hayes laments, "the journalistic bias is geared toward the family next door."

Even though most homeless drunks and drug users will never qualify as the Brady Bunch, the temptation to dismiss them as undeserving is shortsighted. Unlike families that end up in shelters, public inebriates and addicts normally remain homeless for months and sometimes years, soaking up taxpayer dollars in jail and detox units. One recent study of 43 randomly selected recidivist alcoholics in Hennepin County, Minn., found that the annual cost of maintaining the inebriates in various institutions amounted to about $23,000 per client. Moreover, they drink enormous amounts of liquor virtually every day, and because of their chemical dependency on alcohol or drugs often have less control over their lives than many homeless families do.

That seems to be the problem that Americans are not yet ready to confront. The public is clearly more sympathetic to alcoholics and drug abusers who are rich and famous than to those who tug on the sleeves of passers-by for a handout. Still, pollsters repeatedly find that Americans feel guilty that the homeless problem persists. What the conscience-stricken need to understand is that addicts living in the streets need just as much help as the celebrities treated at the Betty Ford clinic.

WHY I AM HOMELESS: HARD LESSONS IN SUPPLY AND DEMAND[3]

In 1986, I joined the ranks of the homeless, forced there by the influx of the new and younger agricultural workers admitted to the United States under the Immigration and Naturalization Reform Act of 1986. At first, I thought the act would be a good thing, but then I found myself being squeezed out of the farm jobs that I have been doing in the Imperial Valley of California since returning from Korea in the 1950s.

The only good thing the Immigration Reform Act has accomplished is its sanctions against employers who hire illegal aliens. The act should have opened up jobs for local citizens and legal aliens. But with the amnesty provisions under Group I and Group II of the act, literally hundreds of thousands of new people have been let into this country to work in the fields on ninety-day permits. Many of them haven't gone any further north than Calexico and other border towns in search of jobs. When the ninety days are over, they go to their first appointment with the INS [Immigration and Naturalization Service] and may or may not receive permits that allow them to continue to work in the United States. These ninety-day entrants have swollen the ranks of the farm workers, taking jobs formerly held by U.S. citizens and legal aliens. Those citizens who are displaced turn to unemployment aid, receiving twenty-six weeks of benefits. After their unemployment insurance runs out, many of them go on welfare and food stamp programs.

Some of the people who come in on Group II permits are not finding work or returning to their former employers but instead are swelling the ranks of the homeless by living on the streets and eating in the soup kitchens. They have found out how much easier it is to live on the street in the United States than in their native Mexico.

[3]Article by C. C. Bruno, who has been a marine, coalminer, mountain brewmaster, carnival roustabout, deckhand, log choker, tractor driver, fieldhand, fruitpicker, baker, and construction worker. From *The Humanist* 49:10+ My/Je '89. Copyright © 1989 by The American Humanist Association. Reprinted with permission.

There are chronic abusers who use up all their benefits under one program and just move on to the next program, town, or shelter. Some abuse the food stamp program by selling their stamps on the street for perhaps half of their value and use that cash to support their vices. In Imperial County, a single male qualifies for ninety dollars a month in food stamps—that is, if he has a permanent residence or address. What happens if his un-employment runs out? He is forced out of his hotel room or apartment, and he goes into the street with his few belongings and basic necessities for survival.

I found it hard to get along on California's minimum wage of $4.25 an hour, even when I worked forty hours a week. Minimum rent was three hundred dollars a month, and there was food and clothing. In Calexico, the last low-cost working-man's hotel was closed this past December, and there are no soup kitchens. Catho-lic Charities have a place where you can stay for thirty days, but it is usually filled up by the ninety-day permit workers. Many men live across the border in Mexicali where the rent is cheaper. But I, for one, don't like the idea of being forced to live in Mexico in order to survive in the United States. So I sleep in the park. Sometimes I find a safe place alongside of the railroad yard or in a little-used alley.

When I go north in California, work is scarce and I have to rely on soup kitchens and shelters. To me, shelter is most impor-tant. I can usually find something to eat behind food markets by going through the dumpsters for discarded vegetables or by pick-ing up aluminum cans and selling them for a few cents to buy a loaf of bread and some bologna. It seems that in this country the powers-that-be have turned against the working man, especially those who have had their roots cut off by some bureaucratic prac-tice that forces them into the homeless classification. How can a man rent a place to live now that the old hotels and rooming houses have been torn down because of some zoning change or because repairing them to meet new building codes is too expensive?

I used to live in the labor camps run by the catering contrac-tors or by the harvesting companies, but even those have been abandoned, and the ones that are still operating charge so much that, with the four or five hours one gets to work, you can vir-tually go into debt living there.

I remember the old Englund labor camps. They were all along the West Coast in the major agricultural areas. Starting in the Imperial Valley, I could follow the harvest all the way to Washington, moving from one camp to another as we finished the harvest. By fall, I always had some money saved to live on until work started again in the Imperial Valley. But not now. Now I am lucky if I can make it to the nearest soup kitchen.

I am reminded of a scene from the movie *The Grapes of Wrath*, which I saw in the late 1940s. It was about migrant workers who moved into a camp run by the state. Why can't our government now come up with a similar program, charging rent according to income? Since governmental agencies are condemning all the affordable housing, they should create something to take its place. There are many single men and women who would be more than willing to move into a place like that.

I have been asked why you don't see more American field workers. Some of the Mexican workers have been heard to comment that it is because the white American male is lazy, that he won't do this type of work. For one thing, most labor contractors are Hispanic and hire accordingly. Citizens and legal aliens are being replaced by the imported aliens. Men from seventeen to sixty years old are willing and able to work. So why let these aliens in to take the jobs? I am personally of the opinion that, given the right incentives, American laborers will do this work. There is need for low-cost housing, particularly for single people, a decent wage so they can afford housing, food, and clothing, and some measure of dignity so they don't have to stand in line to go to church in order to have a bed for the night. This would take a large percentage of the unmarried homeless off the streets.

What are the people doing wrong who are talking about providing housing? They are overlooking the individuals out there. They say, "Help them to help themselves." The majority of the people on the street are not families but single people. They are overlooking that, so they build government-subsidized housing for families. The Department of Housing and Urban Development (HUD) says the only single males who can apply are those disabled or over sixty-five years old.

At one time when I was on unemployment, I received sixty-two dollars a week. I could also apply for food stamps because I was making less than six hundred dollars a month, but, because I had no address, I was denied the stamps. I was also told that they would subtract any wages I made over twenty-five dollars a week from the amount of food stamps I could get. All that you earn over twenty-five dollars a week is discounted from your weekly unemployment. For example, if you make thirty-four dollars gross in a work-week, less twenty-five dollars allowed, they discount the nine dollars from your unemployment wages. If you work more days in that work-week, they subtract all those wages from your unemployment also.

I have met many men in the day centers, soup kitchens, and shelters who aren't agricultural workers. Some of them are printers, electricians, carpenters, and construction workers who, through loss of job, unemployment benefits, and their welfare assistance or because of some "catch-22" regulation, have joined the ranks of the homeless in order to survive.

Ever since the government has become more aware of homelessness, it has made some grants available to those people and organizations which can show a definite need and are able to start pilot programs. Fortunately, there are more people getting involved in trying to take care of the immediate survival needs of the homeless. Other agencies are digging into our educational and welfare systems and are looking into the alcohol and drug abuse programs and land bank subsidies. Who knows, they might yet find solutions to the problems of homelessness.

DON'T SLEEP IN THE SUBWAY—BEGGARS BEWARE: CITIES CRACK DOWN ON VAGRANTS[4]

Brother, can you spare a buck? As public tolerance for the homeless wears thin, cities are trying to control panhandling. [Here are five recent examples from around the nation:]

Atlanta: An Image Problem

Atlanta, the host-designate for the 1996 Olympics, considers itself the Mecca of the New South. But how magnetic can a city be, business people ask, with an estimated 10,000 homeless people scattered around town? Mayor Maynard Jackson proposed a

[4]Article by James N. Baker, from *Newsweek* 117:26 Je 24 '91. Copyright © 1991 by Newsweek, Inc. Reprinted with permission.

"public nuisance" law last week to give police broad powers to arrest beggars and to sweep the homeless from vacant buildings and parking lots. Jackson believes panhandlers alienate visitors, and police say that drug dealers take over buildings occupied by the homeless. Homeless advocates plan to fight back, but they know public sympathy is fading. "To see poor, raggedy homeless people," says Constance Curry, Atlanta's former director of human services, "irritates people now."

New York: Underground Maneuvers

The sidewalks of New York are safe for panhandling, but beggars beware the subway. Plagued by subway crime, transit police have cracked down on vagrants who beg in stations or on trains. How does ejecting the homeless prevent crime? Transit officials believe that if someone with mugging on his mind sees police hassling panhandlers, he thinks twice. It may be working. In the first three months of 1991, officers booted 28,000 vagrants from the subway, a big jump from 3,600 in the same period last year; in a six-month period, ending in April, subway felonies dropped by 16 percent.

San Francisco: Cards Not Cash

Last April, San Francisco's political leaders were shaken by a public-opinion poll. Conducted by the city attorney's office, the poll showed that 25 percent of Bay Area residents, turned off by panhandlers, shop in town less often. So officials proposed an alternative handout: a card that tells a homeless person where to go for help. Advocates are outraged. "It's downright deceitful," says Anthony Vondermuhll of the Coalition on Homelessness, who believes it perpetuates a myth that the city has adequate programs. If the plan goes through, police will refer beggars to agencies, too, instead of arresting them.

Miami: Windshield Patrols

No one walks in Miami, which makes it hard to be a beggar. Instead, the homeless gather at highway exits and offer to clean windshields. Drivers, especially women traveling alone, don't like it. So, in 1989, Dade County outlawed window washing, and Miami assigned a three-officer unit to hunt down offenders. Says a police spokesperson: "We take them to the county jail, which just releases them, and they walk back two or three miles and start again."

Las Vegas: The Tourist Factor

"Las Vegas is probably the meanest city . . . in terms of how it treats its homeless," says Stephen Switzer of the Homeless Advocacy Project. "Casinos don't want anything tampering with tourists spending money." Switzer may be overstating the case, but Vegas officials make no secret of their determination to keep beggars off the Strip. Last spring a federal judge declared an anti-vagrancy law unconstitutional, but officials enforce other statutes, such as trespassing laws, to move the homeless out of sight. The Vegas plan, like the others, offers only a cosmetic fix: vagrants may be cleared off the main streets for a while, but the homeless problem won't go away.

IV. PIERCING THE MYTH: MOVING TOWARD SOLUTIONS

EDITOR'S INTRODUCTION

Although they have been slow in coming, strategies for addressing homelessness and related issues have begun to appear. Part of the difficulty is that no one single approach can possibly encompass the divergent needs of the varied segments of the homeless population. Up to this point, nonprofit and charitable organizations have been the vanguard of programs that are in place. Funding from all levels of government has ranged from insufficient to nonexistent. With the rate of homelessness showing no signs of slowing and its causes becoming more pronounced, the limits of volunteerism are being taxed beyond the breaking point.

Hope does exist though. The articles in this section outline both general strategies and specific programs that may prove effective in the fight against homelessness. Key to their success must be a new resolve by the public and government to deal with root causes of homelessness rather than to employ cosmetic solutions.

The first article, reprinted from *The Economist*, describes approaches that offer some hope of success, as well as federal and local government efforts to control homelessness. Revisiting two articles begun earlier in this book, John J. DiIulio, Jr. writing in *The New Republic* and Sally Reed and R. Craig Sautter writing in *Phi Delta Kappan* propose plans of attack on homelessness with respect to the indigent and mentally ill and in dealing with children. Professor DiIluio outlines programs for the general homeless population, asserting that these must confront the physical health issues affecting all the homeless, but must also provide a resource net of services to address the problems associated with homelessness, especially substance abuse and mental illness. He also suggests government leadership and initiative are necessary to organize the efforts of countless groups working to end or abate homelessness and to provide direction to everyone's efforts. Meanwhile, the *Phi Delta Kappan* report suggests that a primary step to erradicating homelessness overall and, in particular, as it affects children, is to raise the national minimum wage to a level that can sustain shelter and food. Funding of federal programs, like Head Start, and local initiatives by schools and parents can break the cycle of poor education associated with homeless children. The authors also provide examples of programs that work. Together these changes will provide both short- and long-term solutions to phase out the conditions of poverty that spur homelessness.

Nancy Gibbs, writing for *Time* along with Melissa Ludtke and James Willwerth lists a series of programs that have proven successful in treating a variety of the problems of homelessness. Linked to the needs of each community's homeless and aimed at more than just the need for housing, a web of social programs addresses a wider array of homeless problems through enlightened planning, private sector assistance, flexible services, and a system for returning the formerly homeless to society.

The lack of affordable housing has been one cornerstone of the plague of homelessness witnessed in the past decade. Rand Wilson and Mark Sommer offer not a solution but relief from the high cost of building new housing by presenting prefab and modular construction as options employed successfully in several low-income community projects around the country. Writing in *Technology Review* the authors note also that even more economical is the rehabilitation of existing buildings to provide needed relief for the housing shortage. Federal funding, which had been drastically cut in recent years, is the third leg of the problem the author's feel needs to be addressed.

Finally, an article from *The Humanist* by F. Barton Harvey examines how the combined efforts of business, government, and volunteers has made an impact in combating homelessness. Recounting the work of James Rouse in establishing the Enterprise Foundation, Mr. Harvey, himself a member of the Foundation's board of directors and a trustee, cites examples of successful efforts by this group in producing housing around the country. The article identifies the self-sufficient tenant management of these projects as one source of the success. This philosophical reliance on self-sufficiency has also been translated into efforts to help tenants find work, thereby giving them the wherewithal to maintain a home. Although the combination of corporate and state and local government funding, has enabled the program to grow, the article concludes with the admonition that more federal intervention is needed to reverse the trend in which federal housing subsidies have been drastically cut over the past decade.

AMERICAN SURVEY: ROUGHER
AND TOUGHER[1]

George Bush's "kinder, gentler" America has yet to show its face to the homeless. Over the course of a decade, shock at the mounting numbers of "street people" has given way to weariness, and now to intolerance. Across the country hard-pressed local politicians are taking harsh measures to clear the homeless from city streets. Everywhere there is a change of mood, as if the homeless had outworn their welcome.

In New York the city has . . . evicted encampments of the homeless from Tompkins Square Park on Manhattan's lower east side and [from] Columbus Circle. Chicago's O'Hare airport has been closed to the homeless. Santa Barbara has banned sleeping on public streets, and Atlanta's mayor, concerned about the image of his Olympic city, has proposed a bill that would impose criminal penalties (including, absurdly, fines of up to $1,000) for aggressive begging.

Using policemen rather than social workers to deal with the homeless means attacking the symptoms of the problem, while deferring a search for the cure. For Joe Suburb, fed up with picking his way around the slumped bodies on the floor of the railway station, and for Jane Suburb who does not shop in the centre of town any more because beggars frighten her—the symptoms matter. The cure, which might involve higher taxes, seems less urgent. . . .

Inevitably, liberals and conservatives differ over the causes of homelessness. Liberals point to the growth in numbers during the 1980s and blame ungenerous public policy. Conservatives are more likely to argue that homelessness reflects social troubles—drug abuse, the decline of the family—exacerbated by misguided

[1]Article from *The Economist* 320:A21+ Je 29 '91. Copyright © 1991 by The Economist Newspaper, Inc., Ltd. Reprinted with permission.

social policies, like the release of psychiatric patients from hospitals into "community care".

Both have a point. Conservatives are right to argue that simply building more cheap housing and helping more poor people to pay their rent will not solve the problems of the mentally disturbed or the drug-addicted. Surveys of shelter-dwellers suggest that around a third of them suffer from severe psychiatric problems, independent of the strains of living on the street; 40% or so are likely to be regular drug-takers.

Community care for the mentally ill has proved to be a chimera. Too many vulnerable people were left to drift in big cities. As psychiatric hospitals have emptied so prisons have filled—many of the mentally ill may simply have swapped one form of incarceration for another. About 10% of homeless people are former prison inmates.

But the argument that the homeless are more deranged than unlucky is contradicted by history. The policy of letting inmates out of psychiatric institutions—deinstitutionalisation—began in the 1950s, after the discovery that behaviour-modifying drugs could enable many to lead relatively normal lives outside asylums. It had been going on for a generation when the homeless population began to grow so noticeably in the early 1980s. Similarly, the drug problem, though greatly worsened by the arrival of cheap crack in the 1980s, existed before the rise in homelessness. Something else must have happened.

Several trends—some to do with public policy, others with changes in the economy—had begun to converge by the time of the 1981–82 recession. A housing shortage was one element; but it was not caused by the government. The pace of public-housing construction actually increased during the Reagan years: in 1977–80 just over 10,000 units of public housing were built every year; in 1981–88 more than 20,000 were.

More Houses, Fewer Homes

Nonetheless, a shortage of affordable housing did emerge in 1980s. As the public sector built small amounts of low-income housing, so the private sector knocked much greater quantities down. For many years most American cities had their "Skid Rows"—poor areas full of insalubrious hotels and hostels providing cheap, long-term accommodation for single people. . . .

Federal policy did exacerbate the threat of poverty. Changes in welfare laws in 1981 meant that 250,000 families with children lost their right to public assistance. Although various forms of public help, like food stamps, disability payments, welfare and the programmes run by many states remain available to many of the homeless, they are difficult for rootless street dwellers to collect.

The homeless problem has four main ingredients: housing, poverty, drugs and mental illness. Solving one alone will not help much. Building more cheap housing, as Los Angeles plans to do, may help to ease the pressure in a tight housing market—but can be irrelevant in a depressed city like Detroit. Getting a crack addict off drugs will not be enough if he has no job and nowhere to live. Putting the same person into an apartment without dealing with his drug problem is also unlikely to work—or to please the neighbours.

Recognising this, some cities have been drawn towards the idea of "one-stop shopping"—public facilities which will provide shelter and help in the same place. Many of the old shelters are frightening , barracks-like hangars where the homeless spend an uneasy night before being turned out on the streets again the following day. San Francisco, whose mayor, Art Agnos, used to be a social worker, has established a new style of shelter where the "guests" are provided not just with a bed but with daily services from social workers, drug counsellors, job-training experts, lawyers and officials who can identify what type of public benefit a particular person might be eligible for.

The Bush administration, in the shape of the Department of Housing and Urban Development [HUD], is also drawn to this approach. Anna Kondratas, the HUD assistant secretary with direct responsibility for the homeless, points to a new programme—"Shelter Plus Care"—in which the federal government makes housing aid for cities conditional on the provision of social services. The administration is putting some money behind its new policies. Federal funding for programmes to help the homeless has increased from $603m during the last year of the Reagan administration to $884m during the current fiscal year.

But the cities themselves have to bear most of the burden of caring for the homeless on their streets—and many cities are going bust. New York's mayor, David Dinkins, campaigned on a promise to establish "rescue centres" for the homeless, similar to those in San Francisco. Early results were promising. Smaller shelters, specialising in, for example, mentally ill women, have helped to rehouse a high proportion of their charges. But New

York's budget crisis is forcing the city to dismantle its programme. Nine of its 12 small shelters for women will be closed under the latest budget plan—forcing 800 displaced women back into one giant shelter or on to the streets, and closing other shelters for men.

Back at HUD, Mrs Kondratas refuses to be downhearted at what she terms the "consolidation" of the shelter system in New York. The federal government is as broke as the cities. But Mrs Kondratas believes that the number of homeless people has stabilised and can be reduced. She also recognises that Washington has a part to play. "The Reagan administration did not really recognise homelessness as a federal problem," she says. "We do."

THERE BUT FOR FORTUNE[2]

[The first part of this article appears in Section Two of this compilation.]

Confronting the problem of the mentally ill clearly will have to play a part in solutions to homelessness. *Under the Safety Net* describes one program based on the acknowledgment of the dispiriting fact that the incidence of serious mental and physical health problems (such as AIDS, alcoholism, substance abuse, tuberculosis, and hypertension) among homeless Americans is indeed far higher than in the population at large. Making no pretense to solving the fundamental economic problems of the homeless (decent jobs, adequate housing), the Health Care for the Homeless Program (HCHP) addressed itself forthrightly to the vital services needs of unhoused men, women, and children. Supported by the Pew Charitable Trusts and the Robert Wood Johnson Foundation, which invested $25 million in the program in 1983, HCHP was "a five-year experiment in community coalition building and health care innovation" that became an umbrella for programs in nineteen big cities across the nation designed to "provide health care and help in arranging social services—e.g., drug and alcohol treatment programs, public assistance, food stamps, Medicaid,

[2]Article by John J. DiIulio Jr., from *The New Republic* 204:27+ Je 24 '91.
Copyright © 1991 by The New Republic, Inc. Reprinted with permission.

and other entitlements—to otherwise unserved homeless
people." No systematic evaluation of HCHP's effectiveness in helping the homeless has been conducted, but the available evidence is
encouraging, and similar (though much smaller-scale) programs
are now under way.

And meaningful private efforts to help the homeless need not
be the sole province of big foundations and other established
organizations. *What You Can Do to Help the Homeless*, a 123-page
pamphlet produced by the National Coalition to End Homelessness, contains concise practical advice (and gentle moral ex-
hortation) about how one can organize a food drive, tutor homeless children, give special help to battered women, and much
more.

Still, merely raising social consciousness (or social guilt) will
not raise a roof over the heads of the homeless. Private individuals, advocacy groups, charities, churches, and foundations
have been unable to make more than an inspiring dent in the
problem. The time has come for federal, state, and local governments to focus their energies on the homeless. What's needed is a
limited, multifront war on poverty in which each level of government contributes what it can, rather than trading accusations
about passing the buck; too much time has been wasted with the
states charging that the federal government has burdened them
with the problem, and cities, burdened in their turn, claiming
they can't do it alone.

Given the multiple sources of homelessness, efforts to address
the problem will necessarily be a hybrid array of economic assistance and social services, federal leadership and local initiative,
social innovation and judicial reform. In the 1980s, as the problem grew worse, political debates over whose responsibility it was
to help the homeless grew louder, not more constructive, and
debates over the extent and causes of homelessness became more
esoteric, not more useful. The simple lesson for the 1990s is that
such debates do not put a roof over anyone's head. Although
government did not create, and cannot cure, all aspects of the
problem, it can help to solve them. Let's start with the feds.

Without delay both ends of Pennsylvania Avenue should meet
to expand funding for the network of programs operated under
the Stewart B. McKinney Homelessness Act of 1987. In fiscal year
1990 the McKinney Act funneled some $667 million in aid to the
homeless through the Departments of Labor, Education, Health
and Human Services, and HUD [Department of Housing and Ur-

ban Development]. Between 1987 and 1991, most McKinney Act programs provided supplemental funding for ongoing federal initiatives to accelerate or upgrade health care services to the poor. It also established the Health Services for the Homeless program (known formally as Section 340 of the Public Health Service Act). Hundreds of thousands of homeless persons across the country have been served by McKinney-funded health and social services programs. On its way out of the White House, the Reagan administration requested only 15 million [Fiscal Year] 1990 McKinney dollars for health programs, a funding level that would have resulted in the termination of services to 165,000 homeless men, women, and children who had just gained access to health care. But the Bush administration increased that to $63 million and preserved health care for the homeless.

Federal agencies that administer McKinney-funded programs are now engaged in formal evaluations of the act's effectiveness. To date, over a third of all McKinney dollars have gone for housing assistance programs administered by HUD through municipalities and nonprofit organizations. Surely it's worth assessing these and other McKinney programs to see whether they have efficiently delivered help to the greatest possible number of homeless citizens. Based on the existing evidence, however, it is pretty clear that McKinney programs represent federal anti-poverty policy at its best, programs in which "throwing money at the problem" works. Throw more.

While expanding the McKinney safety net, federal policy-makers should also work to fulfill the broader promises of the National Affordable Housing Act, adopted [in] November [1990] with strong bipartisan support as the first major piece of federal housing legislation since the Housing and Community Development Act of 1974. Key provisions of the act are intended to give state and local governments and community-based nonprofit organizations greater discretion in using federal funds to address the problems of affordable housing and homelessness. Unfortunately, this potentially historic legislation is now in danger of becoming just another pawn of Washington partisan in-fighting.

The act, which is administered by HUD, encompasses such programs as HOME, an affordable housing block grant program for states and cities; Shelter Plus Care, which combines two existing housing programs with a new five-year rental assistance program for homeless people who are mentally ill, substance abusers, or in dire need of other social services (recipients match federal contributions dollar for dollar); and HUD Secretary Jack Kemp's pet project, HOPE [Homeownership and Opportunity for People Everywhere], a home ownership program for low-income residents of public housing.

But as interpreted by the Bush administration, the act does not support an expansion in the supply of public housing; indeed, the administration has shifted some public housing construction funds into the HOME block grant. Democrats in Congress have complained bitterly about how HUD is steering the act's implementation, accusing it of selling off public housing, selling out the poor, and failing to pour federal funds into the construction of badly needed new public housing units.

In a recent *Washington Post* op-ed piece, Kemp retorted that the Democrats "cling to programs that transfer income, not assets, to the poor" and give low-income families "just enough aid to lock them in perpetual dependence and despair, but never the incentives or the property needed to achieve full economic freedom." The HOME program, he asserted,

would help 37,000 families within eighteen months, compared to only 7,000 units of public housing that would be built five years from now under current law. When public housing has more than 100,000 vacant units that now go unused by anyone except drug dealers, it is hard to justify building more.

Kemp, who virtually everyone agrees has his heart (if not his HUD) in the right place on poverty issues, is smart enough to know that the mere existence of vacant, drug-infested public housing units no more argues against producing new units than the existence of auto junkyards argues against producing new cars. For their part, congressional Democrats should stop arguing that simply constructing more units nationwide at federal expense is the answer. It's not.

Both the administration and its congressional critics should take the federalism logic of the National Affordable Housing Act seriously enough to recognize that some jurisdictions probably do need enhanced federal support for more public housing units, other jurisdictions probably don't; and the need for new units will vary from place to place and across time according to demographic and other changes that are hard to predict but can be estimated. At the same time, the administration needs to be much more practical about the difficulties of implementing long-term solutions to poverty and homelessness such as making public housing tenants into homeowners. A recent article in *National*

Journal noted that the bill for "empowerment" at Kemp's show-place, the Kenilworth-Parkside neighborhood in Washington D.C., now stands at $130,000 per apartment (residents must have a job or be in job-training to qualify for one), and many other homeownership projects have been mired in cost overruns and delays. Under the act, balancing such programs as HOME, Shelter Plus Care, and HOPE with new construction where necessary would constitute a winning federal housing policy for the homeless.

Independent of federal initiatives, state governments can do at least two things to combat homelessness. First, they can improve the quality of state-funded total-care institutions for the mentally ill, and pass laws designed to protect the civil rights of the homeless mentally ill against those who, in the name of civil liberties, would sentence mentally incompetent fellow citizens to a life of misery. Making possible the involuntary commitment of the chronically mentally ill would not greatly reduce the total number of homeless, but it would greatly reduce the amount of human suffering compounded by homelessness.

Second, responsible state officials can take greater pains in regulating local shelters. As it now stands, some shelters are clean; others are filthy. Some are violence-ridden; others are not. Some offer basic services and amenities; others do not. Recently, for example, New York's State Department of Social Services investigated conditions inside New York City's shelter system and found numerous violations of state regulations, including overcrowded and unsanitary living conditions that posed a serious risk to homeless women and children. But the state's response was a threat to cut its substantial financial support for the city's shelters, which would only make things worse.

In all such cases, a better response would be for the state to force the offending locality to bring its shelters up to standard. And if elected and appointed state officials prove unable or un-willing to do so, state or federal judges should step in. Court intervention into the administration of public institutions (pris-ons, schools, mental hospitals) is rarely an unqualified success, but a homeless New Yorker in a public shelter is a worthier object of activist attentions than a criminal New Yorker in a Riker's jail.

Local government officials have never waited for state or federal direction to help the homeless. According to the U.S. Conference of Mayors report, in many localities most funding for homeless assistance programs comes from locally generated revenues rather than from state or federal grants. Even near-broke big cities can learn from each other's experiences with the homeless and do more on at least three fronts. First, on a jurisdiction-by-jurisdiction basis, municipal housing codes and regulations need to be reviewed and, where necessary, revised in order to increase the stock of affordable housing and low-income rental units. Given Mayor Dinkins's recent insights on the subject, New York City ought to lead the way. The extensive and expensive safety (as well as aesthetic) standards now written into many urban housing codes have had the effect of regulating out of existence the construction and rental of low-cost conventional dwellings, which is a recipe for homelessness.

Second, rather than passing laws to "evict" the homeless from the streets, for a little money (and lots of disinfectant) local authorities can establish public sanitary stations such as Cincinnati's Mary Magdalene House, where the homeless can use a toilet, grab a shower, wash their clothes, and make phone calls. And even municipalities that are drenched in red ink can afford to be more supportive of the private (often church-based) groups that are doing a lot to help the homeless on very scarce funds.

Third, local leaders throughout the country should repeat recent experiments made in Philadelphia, Seattle, Atlanta, and other cities with "self-governing" shelters in which the homeless assume responsibility for everything from preparing meals to keeping the place clean and orderly. Philadelphia's Food For Life shelter, for example, even has some former residents now working on its staff. There is absolutely no reason why public shelters should be horrible places, horribly run. Nobody thinks shelters are an ideal answer. But the lesson of the last decade is that they aren't mere emergency measures either. The time has come to think seriously about how best to maintain them. Many observers believe that empowering the homeless to take charge of shelters serves as a vital first step on the road to their economic and personal recovery. Let's find out.

"Homeless American" is a moral oxymoron, but most of us have yet to understand it that way. As an unspoken moral precept for civic action, "blessed are the poor" has lost its sway. Our civic failure here cannot be measured in the number of public assistance tax dollars spent or withheld, or the amount of pocket change given or kept. All such failures are at once communal and individual, profound moral accidents at that intersection of private interest and public spirit known as citizenship. For several months now I've been searching for Willie Brown, hoping that he's alive and well, and praying that my old friend, if he ever did become homeless, met with better fellow citizens than me.

CHILDREN OF POVERTY[3]

[The first part of this article appears in Section Two of this compilation.]

What Society Must Do

No single individual or group can successfully tackle all the factors that contribute to child poverty. The lack of jobs that pay a decent wage, for example, is the biggest contributor to poverty in small towns, cities, and suburbs. Clearly, this is a national problem that can be addressed only by a comprehensive economic policy that gives top priority to the creation of jobs that pay a living wage. A number of family experts believe that an even greater increase in the minimum wage than the one recently passed by Congress is essential to help the working poor escape a lifetime of poverty.

Some effective programs already exist to deal with almost every aspect of the cycle of child poverty. But the programs that work have never been properly funded. Head Start is the classic example. Head Start was created by the antipoverty legislation of the 1960s, and a number of studies have documented its positive impact. One study found that nearly 60% of the Head Start graduates were employed at age 19, compared to just 32% of a control group. Only 49% of the control group had graduated from high school, while 67% of the former Head Start students had earned high school diplomas. Nearly 40% of the Head Start graduates had taken some college courses, while just 21% of the control group had taken any coursework beyond high school.

Such statistics add up to lives and money saved. One dollar invested in Head Start saves $7 in later social services that are not

[3]Article by Sally Reed and R. Craig Sautter, from *Phi Delta Kappan* 71:K1+ Je '90. Copyright © 1990 by Phi Delta Kappa, Inc. Reprinted with permission.

needed. Numbers of this kind have convinced many, but Head
Start . . . still serves only one in five eligible students.

That situation might be about to change. There are hopeful
signs that some basic services for poor children could improve in
the next few years if the federal government reasserts its leadership in child care, health coverage, and education. . . .

Educators worry that, as the number of children in poverty
grows, education for those children—without sharp increases in
funding for Chapter 1 and Head Start—can only get worse, not
better. Susan Frost, executive director of the Committee for Education Funding, says that "there is no alternative to Chapter 1 and
Head Start, which are estimated to serve only one-half and one-
fifth respectively of eligible children." The needs of such children, she adds, are not going to be met by restructuring.

Meanwhile, there is growing public support for offering a
wider array of social and health services in the schools. In September 1989 a survey by the *Washington Post* and ABC News
found widespread support for a variety of nontraditional services
in the schools: the dissemination of information about birth control, counseling for psychiatric and drug-related problems, more
nutrition information, and so on. Likewise, the 21st Annual Gal-
lup Poll of the Public's Attitudes Toward the Public Schools found
74% of the public willing to spend more tax dollars to screen
children for health programs, 69% willing to spend more money
for Head Start, and 58% willing to spend more for day care for
young children whose parents work.

What Schools Can Do

The prevalence of child poverty in the U.S. is enough to make
any educator shudder—and not just because of the damage to the
children. All too often the public schools are given the burden of
overcoming economic and social inequities, usually without adequate resources to confront these difficult problems. Indeed, children who have been maimed by such new social epidemics as
homelessness and crack use by pregnant women are already testing the resources and tolerance of the schools. Many reformers
believe that, instead of another add-on program, the schools need
a coordinated and concerted societal effort to deal with these
problems.

Still, all across the nation, educators are struggling to meet the
crisis with innovative solutions and more of their legendary dedi-

cation. The many examples of their efforts fall into two major categories: mobilizing parents and integrating community and health resources into the school.

Parent Involvement

Some educators are reexamining the roles parents can play in the schools. But poor parents face significant obstacles to becoming involved. According to the National Committee for Citizens in Education, "A parent who speaks limited English or who was herself a school dropout is unlikely to volunteer as a member of a school improvement council. A poor parent who has no automobile may not be able to send his child to a better public school located outside the attendance area—even when the option is available—unless transportation is provided by the school district. These barriers to full participation can be removed with training, encouragement, and resources that insure equal access."

Nevertheless, many educators are putting their energies into parent solutions—and getting results.

• The Center for Successful Child Development, known as the Beethoven Project, is a family-oriented early childhood intervention program at the Robert Taylor Homes, a public housing project on the south side of Chicago. Sponsored by the Chicago Urban League and by the Ounce of Prevention Fund, the Beethoven Project opened in 1987. Some 155 families now benefit from a variety of educational, social, and medical services for young children who will ultimately enroll in the Beethoven Elementary School.

• In Missouri, Parents as Teachers combines an early childhood component with an education program for parents. It began as a pilot program in 1981, and today all 543 Missouri school districts are required to provide certain services to families, including parent education, periodic screening through age 4 to detect developmental problems, and educational programs for those 3- and 4-year-olds who are developmentally delayed. The program is not restricted to poor children, but it can catch their problems early, and results have been encouraging.

• James Comer, director of the School Development Program at Yale University, is working with 100 inner-city schools across the country to create management teams made up of parents, teachers, and mental health professionals. The aims are to improve the teachers' knowledge of child development, to involve parents, and to provide children with community resources normally found outside the school.

• In California and Missouri a new approach, known as the Accelerated Schools Program, is trying to change parents' attitudes toward their children. The Accelerated Schools Program attempts to raise parents' expectations about what their children can do, while it also focuses on giving literacy training to the parents. The goal is to empower parents so that they can become involved in their children's education. The program currently operates in two schools in California and in seven schools in Missouri.

A number of researchers and scholars have endorsed the idea of parent involvement. For example, Harold Stevenson of the University of Michigan released a study in 1989 that found that, contrary to popular belief, black and Hispanic mothers are keenly interested in their children's education and want to be involved despite the economic and social barriers to their doing so.

Parents can play a key role in many aspects of a school, providing a sense of community that can nurture as well as protect children in a school setting. During a cold Boston winter, for example, parents noticed that some children at David A. Ellis School in Roxbury did not have warm jackets. The parents established a clothing exchange to make sure that the children were warm on their way to school.

"The parents are part of the everyday life of the school," says Owen Haleem of the Institute for Responsive Education (IRE) at the Boston University School of Education. Two years ago the IRE organized a Schools Reaching Out Project. In January 1990 it organized a national network to increase parent and community involvement in urban public schools serving low-income communities. Known as the League of Schools Reaching Out, the network now includes 37 schools in 19 urban school districts.

"New relationships with low-income parents must be fashioned in order to break the link between poverty and school failure," according to Don Davies, president of the IRE. Two schools were part of a two-year pilot study of ways to develop these new relationships. The David A. Ellis School in Roxbury and Public School 111 in District 2 on the west side of Manhattan each converted one classroom near the principal's office into an on-site parents' center and initially paid a full-time "key teacher" to serve as a link between the school, the students' families, and the community. P.S. 111 offered classes in English as a second language (ESL) for Spanish-speaking parents and organized a lending library for educational toys and games. Parents at Ellis School offered ESL and formed a support group to study for the high-school-equivalency exams. Both schools send trained parents and community members to visit other parents at home and organize collaborative projects between teachers and parents.

The IRE pilot study was modeled, in part, on a similar program in Liverpool, England, where each school has a coordinator of social services. The IRE programs at P.S. 111 and at Ellis School try to combat the idea that parents need only to come to school for meetings. According to Haleem, "Our goal was to work with regular public schools to build fundamentally different relationships with low-income parents." And both schools have recorded achievement gains, which, Haleem notes, may not be connected to the parent involvement program. But then again they might be.

To some child advocates, *family* literacy is the key both to involving parents and to improving student achievement. A Department of Defense study conducted in the 1980s found that the most important variable in determining the educational attainment of 16- to 23-year-olds was the educational level of their mothers. Indeed, Thomas Sticht of Applied Behavioral and Cognitive Sciences, Inc., in San Diego argues that federal programs need to work with families.

. . . Even Start, a program of financial assistance to local agencies that conduct projects in family-centered education [has been receiving Department of Education funds]. Privately funded and family-centered literacy projects, such as the Kenan Family Literacy Project in Louisville, Kentucky, also teach basic skills to parents while their children attend a preschool. Operating in seven schools in Kentucky and North Carolina, the Kenan Family Literacy Project teaches parents to read and to teach their children to read. This program was a model for the Foundation for Family Literacy, initiated by First Lady Barbara Bush.

For poor children whose parents remain uninvolved, schools may have to come up with other answers. An increasing number of social scientists argue that just one relationship between an adult and a disadvantaged child in stressful conditions can make a significant difference.

Public/Private Ventures, a nonprofit organization based in Philadelphia, examined five programs involving adults in the community and at-risk students. It found that the bonds that formed between the generations helped the youngsters weather crises, gave them a sense of stability, and improved their sense of their own competence.

Schools as Social Centers

Indeed, many educators feel that they'll be able to address the needs of poor children only if the community works with the schools.

"The most urgent task is to regenerate families deep in the inner cities," Roger Wilkins, a professor of history at George Mason University, argued in the *New York Times* last year. "While employment, early childhood education, and child-care programs are critical parts of such an effort, it is essential that the public schools become the focus of special remedies," Wilkins asserted. "In addition, the schools would become centers of the community for the children they serve and for their parents and grandparents."

Indeed, more and more schools are designing programs that link social services and academic programs. But such ventures require schools and communities to overcome the instinct to protect their own turf and to agree to work together as one entity.

A number of states—including New York, Oregon, South Carolina, and Florida—have initiated new efforts to coordinate services for children. The problem is that child services are so spread out. In California, for example, 160 state programs for children operate out of 45 agencies. Schools must organize the services in ways that funnel them directly toward the complex needs of poor youngsters.

One initiative that helps not only poor children but all children coming of age today was started by Edward Zigler, Sterling Professor of Psychology and director of the Bush Center in Child Development and Social Policy at Yale University. Zigler has touted "Schools for the 21st Century"—schools that function as community centers, linking a host of family-support services to help children overcome social, psychological, and health problems. The approach includes home visitations, assistance for parents with infants, day care for 3- to 5-year-olds, before- and after-school care for school-age children, teen pregnancy prevention programs, and adult literacy classes. Zigler's program began in Independence, Missouri, and has spread to five states.

One educator who agrees that the school needs to take on a

broader role in the lives of children is Allan Shedlin, Jr. In 1987 the Elementary School Center that Shedlin directs called for a reconceptualization of the elementary school as the locus of advocacy for all children.

"Traditional sources of support for the child—the family, the neighborhood, schools, social and religious organizations, nutritional and health care programs—are fragmented or do not exist at all for many children," says Shedlin. School has become the only agency that deals with every child, every day. Thus the school should serve as the center of advocacy for children.

The National School Boards Association (NSBA) argues that school officials cannot wait until all the desired elements are in place before taking action, and it suggests a number of remedies. Schools should:

• establish a local policy to help all children learn—perhaps by means of counseling programs, tutoring programs, or parent involvement;

• examine the needs of a community and determine whether parents need day-care services, health services, job skills, or the help of volunteers;

• develop a demographic profile of the school system—find out whether families are in poverty and whether there are single-parent families, migrant families, immigrant families—and communicate this information to all people in the school system;

• define and identify all youth at risk—considering such factors as student absenteeism, poor grades, low test scores in math or reading, chemical dependency, boredom, and family mobility;

• follow student progress in school by keeping comprehensive records;

• evaluate programs that have already been implemented;

• give administrators and teachers flexibility in helping students at risk and make use of student mentors, faculty advisors, teaching teams, and tutoring;

• involve parents in children's schooling; and

• work with local businesses, agencies, and organizations to develop and fund programs.

Carol Pringle didn't believe that she could wait only longer to help the poor children in her Seattle community. In April 1989 the mother of three and former schoolteacher organized a two-room schoolhouse called First Place. It is now one of a dozen programs in the country designed for homeless children. Technically it is a nonprofit agency, but it works in cooperation with the Seattle School District, which provides buses each day to round up children (kindergarten through grade 6) from homeless shelters all over the city.

Two salaried teachers and a number of volunteers have adapted the regular school curriculum for this new clientele. But the school also finds shoes for the children and, in addition to basic academics, provides breakfast, lunch, and a safe environment. Students stay an average of four to five weeks, but some attend for only a single day. They come from shelters for battered women or live with mothers who can't afford housing. Some are from families that move constantly in an effort to find work.

Other school systems have different programs. The Harbor Summit School in San Diego is near the St. Vincent de Paul Joan Kroc Center. The Tacoma (Washington) School District and the Tacoma YWCA run the Eugene P. Tone School.

However, some school officials believe that homeless children should not be placed in separate programs. Yvonne Rafferty, director of research with Advocates for Children, claims that all children should be in regular programs. New York City prohibits any separate programs for homeless children, and Minneapolis tries to provide homeless children with transportation to their former school.

Essentially the solution to the problem of schooling for homeless children is a state responsibility. The McKinney Act of 1987 grants money to states to develop plans so that homeless children can gain access to the schools.

Like Carol Pringle, Carol Cole couldn't wait any longer. Just as the first wave of crack babies was hitting school systems across the nation, she was hard at work creating a special program for such children. The Salvin Special Education School in Los Angeles is a two-year-old program designed to aid children born to crack-addicted mothers. Eight 3- and 4-year-olds work with three teachers, who give the children as much individual attention as possible. The school has a pediatrician, a psychologist, several social workers, and a speech and language specialist. According to Cole, the home lives of the children are "chaotic." Salvin School reaches only eight children at a time. But 375,000 drug-exposed babies are born annually.

A survey released by the NSBA in February 1990 found that urban school districts face an "awesome challenge" in trying to provide more social services when federal aid for such programs has declined in real dollars. The survey of 52 urban school districts found that the proportion of resources devoted to attacking social and health programs puts "a severe strain on local school districts' budgets, draining their coffers."

Jonathan Wilson, chairman of the NSBA Council of Urban Boards of Education, argues that local resources are running dry. If urban schools are to improve their performance, he maintains, they need dramatic hikes in state and federal funding and in Chapter 1.

In the end the Children's Defense Fund calculates that the key investments to help rescue children from poverty are not prohibitively expensive. The CDF estimates that universal health care for children and pregnant women is a relatively inexpensive prevention measure and is a far better social policy than trying to remediate social ills later. In addition, the CDF figures that the costs of eliminating poverty and child poverty are not as high as many people think. Good nutrition, basic health care, and early education can make a big difference.

"We must shed the myth that all poor children need massive, long-term public intervention," Marian Wright Edelman told those attending the annual meeting of the CDF in Washington, D.C., in March 1990. "Certainly, some children are so damaged that they need such help," Edelman allows. "But millions of poor children need only modest help. They need child care, not foster care; a checkup, not an intensive-care bed; a tutor, not a guardian; drug education, not detoxification; a scholarship, not a detention cell. But it has been hard to get them what they need—even when we know what to do and when it saves us money."

According to CDF estimates (based on 1987 figures), the cost of eliminating child poverty is $17.22 billion; the cost of eliminating poverty in families with children, $26.874 billion; the cost of eliminating poverty among all persons, $51.646 billion. That last figure is equivalent to only 1% of our gross national product. Eliminating poverty in families with children would cost only about 1.5% of the total expenditures of federal, state, and local governments combined.

Indeed, if the nation's largest bankers are capable of writing off billions of dollars in debts owed by developing nations, if the U.S. Congress can almost nonchalantly commit $325 billion dollars to bailing out the unregulated and marauding savings-and-loan industry, if the public can live with military excesses and a

variety of foreign affairs ventures, then surely we can renegotiate
the terms of the escalating human debt embodied by the children
of poverty.

Congress, the states, and local communities must rewrite the
options of opportunity for *all* our children, but especially for our
poor children. We must be willing to write the checks that guaran-
tee poor children a real chance of success from the moment they
are conceived until the moment that they receive as much education as they can absorb. Only then will the tragedy of children
deprived from birth of a dignified life be banished forever from
this land.

ANSWERS AT LAST[4]

There was a time in public memory when Americans imagined that the homeless were refugees of a kind, on their way from
somewhere to somewhere else, residing temporarily in the tunnels and doorways between here and there. Some people were
uprooted after the War on Poverty was fought to a draw, when
their rents went up, their wages went down, and the safety net
turned out to be full of holes. Others were in transit from mental
asylums that didn't heal them or to halfway houses that didn't
exist. Still others were maimed by drug abuse. Communities from
coast to coast quietly wished that the living clutter would all go
away. Yet during the [1980s] it has only multiplied.

Who could have imagined, in so smugly prosperous a decade,
that shantytowns would become tourist attractions? Until the
mayor evicted them . . . , homeless people in San Francisco drew
busloads of photo-snapping foreign tourists to their refugee
camp in front of city hall. There, the visitors found a second city
of cardboard condos, clogged with the traffic of shopping carts
through makeshift living rooms, outfitted with easy chairs and
dresser drawers. The waterless fountain steamed with stale urine;
a sun-scorched lawn sprouted cigarette butts.

Over the years no social issue has looked so easy and proved
so hard to resolve. It looked easy because merely building houses

[4]Article by Nancy Gibbs, from *Time* 136:44+ D 17 '90. Copyright © 1990 by the
Time Incorporated Magazine Company. Reprinted with permission.

is simpler than, say, curing a deadly disease or cleansing a polluted ocean or handing out hope to the poor. But it turned out to be a nettlesome problem, for homelessness is not the same as houselessness. Each disaster has its own genealogy; the problems of the street people only begin with the need for shelter. Perhaps that is because homelessness is a symptom of every other social ill: drugs, crime, poverty, teenage pregnancy, illiteracy, violence, even the decline of compassion during the me-first '80s.

When the street people first appeared in force a decade or so ago, they inspired shouts of dismay and calls for action. Cities hurriedly opened shelters; churches converted their basements into temporary dormitories; soup kitchens doubled their seating capacity. When the problem only grew worse, city officials across the nation sought to drive beggars from their tunnels and parks and public doorways. The homeless became targets; sleeping vagrants were set afire, doused with acid and, in a particularly horrific attack in New York City last Halloween, slashed with a meat cleaver. Finally came resignation. After years of running hurdles over bodies in train stations, of being hustled by panhandlers on the street, many urban dwellers moved past pity to contempt, and are no longer scalded by the suffering they see.

"Society lost faith that there were solutions," says Paul Grogan, president of the Local Initiatives Support Corporation, a source of funds and faith for grass-roots rescue efforts. A poll by the Marist Institute for Public Opinion shows that 75% of Americans believe the homeless problem will worsen or remain the same. The irony is that the loss of hope has occurred just when hope may be at hand. In city after city, advocates of the homeless can point to programs and policies that are tailormade, cost effective, time tested. Now if adequate funds are provided, they will know what to do with them.

San Francisco could end up setting an example. When last year's earthquake nearly leveled a few crumbling flophouses, the city resisted building the standard emergency homeless shelters. Instead, officials used almost $12 million in federal relief money to build state-of-the-art multiservice centers where homeless people can live, get health care, see a social worker, treat their addictions, receive job training—whatever is necessary to meet their needs and return them to independent living. "If you give me the money, we have the chance to end sleeping on the streets," says Mayor Art Agnos. "I'm willing to be the first mayor in America to say so."

It may seem such an obvious prescription—build housing, and then help people hold on to it. But it has taken a long time to strip homeless policy of its mythology. For years, whenever the congressional committees or the network-news programs took up the cause, they would call Robert Hayes, founder of the National Coalition for the Homeless, and put in an order for an intact white family recently evicted from a Norman Rockwell painting—people, they said, with whom others could identify. Yet in cities like New York, such families account for less than 10% of the homeless population, a tiny proportion compared with the homeless who are drug addicts, ex-convicts, alcoholics, single mothers, mostly black and Hispanic. Homeless advocates admit to a well-intentioned whitewash: in their search for support and sympathy, they conspired to uphold the sanitized image of the deserving poor, in fear that if the more complex truth were known, the public would blame the victims and walk away.

And who could know the truth anyway? Estimates of the number of homeless people have ranged from 300,000 to 3 million. There may never be an accurate national figure. . . . No city is typical. In Norfolk, Va., 81% of homeless people are thought to be families with children; in Minneapolis, 76% are single men, according to the 1989 Conference of Mayors Survey. Nationwide, anywhere from one-half to two-thirds are either substance abusers, mentally ill or both. Up to a quarter have been in jail. With such a great range of needs, it was all but impossible to cook up a comprehensive national policy that would fit into a 10-second sound bite.

So when advocates were pressed for a solution, they answered the congressional committees and task forces and think tanks with a sharp demand: "Housing, housing and housing." And in a way, they were right. It was no secret that a main cause of homelessness in the '80s was the poor being squeezed out of the housing market. In the 1970s and '80s, the average rent grew twice as fast as the average income. Manufacturing jobs disappeared: of the 12 million new jobs created since 1979, more than half pay less than $7,000 a year, and many provide no health insurance. One serious illness, and a worker could spiral into poverty and onto the streets. Meanwhile, a 1981 change in welfare laws meant that a quarter of a million families with children lost all their public assistance, and an additional 200,000 had benefits reduced.

Rising rents in a tight real estate market were enough to cast these borderline workers and welfare families out of their homes. For young people approaching the housing market for the first time, there was no point of entry. In Massachusetts cities, a renter must earn $13.65 an hour—more than three times the minimum wage—to afford the $800-a-month average rent on a two-bedroom unit in decent condition. Under the Reagan Administration, the Federal Government cut housing assistance 75%, and much of what was left was wasted. The Department of Housing and Urban Development stopped subsidizing new housing and handed out rent vouchers instead. This increased demand without increasing the supply and set off a scramble for the cheap units that remained.

When people began to compete fiercely for affordable housing, the ones to lose out were the least resourceful: the teenage mothers, the addicted, the abused, the illiterate, the unskilled. The explosion of crack use in the '80s did immeasurable damage; once people were addicted, what employer or landlord would touch them? "Ronald Reagan and the housing cuts are a convenient way to look at the homeless problem," says Mike Neely, an engineer in Los Angeles, who squandered all he had, including his home and family, on cocaine before he turned his life around and founded the Homeless Outreach Project. "I think it's a drug problem. You can't pay the landlord and the dope man at the same time." . . .

When wave after wave of newly homeless people rolled through the cities, emergency shelters seemed the surest and quickest way to get them off the streets. So most of the money allocated by Congress and by states went toward emergency, rather than preventive, care. Only rarely was there money for rental assistance, tenant-landlord mediation or short-term crisis loans to help the near homeless keep the roofs over their heads. Public money paid slumlords $2,000 a month to put up families in "welfare hotels." But this did nothing to ease the families' desperation, fight their addictions or restore their dignity. The emergency shelters grew up like weeds in the cities because there was no time to plant anything else.

Though they were never supposed to become a part of the landscape, the temporary shelters soon began to look like permanent poorhouses. Architects studied how to build better shelters; interior decorators worked to beautify them. The late Mitch Snyder, the ubiquitous crusader, created a vast Washington shelter that was considered a model of its kind. "It is the best shelter in the world," he once said of his creation, "but it is an abomination and should be destroyed."

Every shelter may be an abomination in theory, but many were in fact as well. Half the people residing for more than two years in New York City shelters test positive for tuberculosis. Men sleep with their shoes wedged under the legs of the cots so they won't be stolen. At least one-third of all homeless women have been raped. "You don't get to sit and relax when you're homeless," says Catherine, 62, a homeless woman in Seattle. . . .

When cities tried to move families out of shelters, they discovered just how deeply scarred the victims were. In an effort to empty its disgraceful welfare hotels, New York City renovated old public housing and moved in homeless families. No one anticipated the invisible quarantine: shunned by their neighbors, the families had no sense of community, no help for the problems that had put them on the streets in the first place. Many parents still had no jobs, still drank too much, still beat their kids. Within a year, some of the buildings had been looted or burned, and drug dealers were moving in. At city-council hearings, tenants testified repeatedly that rehabilitating the buildings was not enough. The city had to "rehab people."

Other cities were having the same experience, until it became impossible to sustain the illusion that all a pregnant, crack-addicted teenage prostitute with AIDS needed was a place to call home. From that admission was born the concept of linkage. Rather than merely providing a shelter, homeless advocates are weaving a web. By combining detoxification programs, job training, day care, parenting classes, health care and social services under one roof, they can help the street people who are unwilling or unable to travel all over town to find the services they need—if those services exist.

Not only are such multipurpose centers more humane than warehousing people in welfare hotels, but they can also cost about half as much. Each city, even each neighborhood, can custom-design its programs. Areas with a desperate AIDS problem can focus on providing outpatient care. For single adults, SROs with on-site services may be a permanent answer. For homeless families, transitional housing can cushion their re-entry into the private market.

In the absence of leadership from Washington, local governments and private groups have spent countless millions of hours and dollars on this problem. Because the homeless population varies so greatly from city to city, community groups often devise the most ingenious solutions—especially when they can enlist the help of corporations, banks and local government. In New York, America Works trains welfare recipients for jobs and pays their salaries for the first four months; if the employer is satisfied and hires a worker permanently (usually about 70% of trainees make it), America Works collects a $5,000 fee from the state. Employers get a trained employee, the state reduces its welfare bill, and the worker becomes self-sufficient.

Leading the private-sector initiative is developer James Rouse's Enterprise Foundation, a sort of brain-trust godparent to housing efforts all across the country. Rouse's idea was to combine government incentives, benign capitalism and community energy to build decent, affordable housing. One key to the organization's success is Rouse's knack for persuading corporations to get involved and for pointing out the tax incentives that make it worth their while. If a company invests $1 million in a financing pool for low-income housing, over 15 years it could realize $2.3 million in tax savings.

But the risk that comes with private success is that it gives the Federal Government an excuse to applaud the local initiatives and then bow out. In Washington itself, with a huge homeless population, private groups are struggling to "hold the situation together with gum and baling wire," says Jack M. White Jr. of the city's Coalition for the Homeless. Even Washington's most ebullient convert to the cause—Housing Secretary Jack Kemp—is full of ideas but inevitably short of funds. His latest initiative, Homeownership and Opportunity for People Everywhere [HOPE], would promote home ownership for low-income tenants and support local nonprofit groups. But its total funding is only $750 million . . . [for 1991]. The 1987 McKinney Act allotted $596 million [in 1990] . . . to states and cities for homeless programs. But even that amount pales next to what the cities are spending. New York City's human-resources administration will spend $146.4 million on the homeless . . . [in 1991]; its portion of McKinney funds . . . [totalled] only $5.95 million.

Finally, perhaps the single greatest source of help for the homeless comes from volunteers. Frustrated, angry, ashamed that a country so wealthy should ignore such poverty, volunteers give money and their time to manning the soup kitchens, supervising the church basements at night, distributing information, teaching reading, running clothing drives. In the process, they are learning invaluable lessons about what works and what does not. For example:

• Go beyond shelter. Providing a roof for the night is not enough, and in many cities the shelters are not full. Homeless people need a place that is safe and that addresses their needs. Drug addicts need treatment; the mentally ill need guidance; single mothers need help with child rearing; most homeless people need job training and health care. Don't make them commute all over town to get it.

• Have a plan. To avoid duplication and red tape, city policymakers and charities must coordinate their efforts. Officials in Portland, Ore., devised a 12-point plan for coordinating services that has been widely copied by other communities. Each city must study its own homeless population to understand its nature and needs, then devise a strategy for solving the problem.

• Involve the private sector. Private corporations allied with pioneering charities can make public money stretch a long way. In 1986–87 some 460 nonprofit community groups created 23,120 units of low-income housing, compared with nearly 20,000 for HUD.

• Build communities. When it is time to move homeless people into permanent housing, do not isolate them. City officials must resist the temptation to congratulate themselves with signs on the buildings, like those that have appeared in New York City, that in essence announce that this is where formerly homeless people live. Homelessness carries a terrible stigma, particularly for children. Its veterans must be allowed to return to the community without carrying that stigma with them.

• Have services, will travel. Even if social services are available, many homeless people cannot or will not use them. So more and more cities are mobilizing their resources. Food vans carry soup and sandwiches to the bridges and parks. Boston's Health Care for the Homeless program sends nurses out knocking on doors in family shelters, offering parents and children preventive health care.

• Build more housing. It is only the start of a solution—but the problem will never be solved without it.

When foreign visitors come to American cities, their reaction is almost invariably astonishment, and sorrow, at what they see on the streets. America is a wealthy nation of conspicuous ideals, one that presumes to have something to teach infant democracies all around the world. By failing to act creatively, generously and mercifully on behalf of its most desperate citizens, a country loses more than its credibility; it weakens its character. After such a long and ambivalent search for answers to this problem, Americans should rejoice that there is at last an opportunity to act on the principles they so proudly proclaim.

It's Christmas in April

Minerva Ketter lost her home gently, over time, as her listing house sank around her. The ceiling let in rain, the floors let in light, and the front porch gradually sagged until it was almost in the front yard. Finally, she had to abandon her ramshackle house and move in with her father next door.

Then one . . . spring [day] volunteers swarmed like carpenter ants over the Hartsville, S.C., neighborhood, slapping paint, hammering walls, shingling roofs, shoring up porches. By day's end, Ketter's house, like 37 others in town, had been delivered from ruin. "I didn't know something like this could happen," marveled Ketter, 34, who is pregnant with her second child. "This will make all the difference in my life."

If it felt to Ketter like Christmas in April, that's because it was. Each spring the Washington-based Christmas in April program coordinates thousands of volunteers in 50 cities and towns from Vermont to California in renovating more than a thousand homes that are near collapse. Better to rebuild old dwellings, they figure, than to build new homeless shelters. In one day of hard work the 1,000 Hartsville volunteers used 400 gal. of paint, 800 lbs. of nails, 7,000 ft. of lumber, 5,000 squares of shingles and 200 bags of cement, all paid for by local donations with an enviable provision: if they fell short, Sonoco Products Co., a plastics-packaging giant acting as sponsor, would write a check for the difference.

For the beneficiaries, the arrival of Christmas in April was a gift beyond measure. Janie and Lyde Hawkins have been married since 1925; theirs was a dismal home, in dire need of a new roof, porch and windows. "We ain't got to pay for it?" Janie asked coordinator Trish Lunn every time she came by.

"No, not one dime," Lunn replied.

"The Lord bless you for that."

Building Transitions to Safety

It is hard to imagine what the owners of Cleveland's abandoned 76-room TraveLodge motel must have thought when Sister Loretta and Sister Donna announced that they wanted to buy what they called a "notorious cathouse." "Sister Donna and I had about $1.98 between us," recalls Sister Loretta. But the two nuns of the Sisters of St. Joseph had other assets, acquired during years of working to help the poor against heavy odds, that they leveraged into a remarkable deal. They managed to raise the $270,000 purchase price from banks, churches, government organizations and James Rouse's Enterprise Foundation—plus an additional $400,000 for renovations. From that unlikely beginning was born Transitional Housing Inc. (THI), a way station for women traveling between emergency shelters and permanent homes.

The nuns knew that many homeless women have trouble moving directly from a shelter into a place of their own, even if apartments are available—and affordable. A few months on the streets can leave a person deeply alienated and frightened of returning to "normal" life. Through self-esteem seminars, employment training, drug counseling and other programs, women are prepared to return to the job market, retrieve children from foster care and set up homes.

More than 400 women have stayed, usually for about 13 months, since THI opened its doors in 1986. Roughly 65% of the cases involved alcohol and drug use, while 85% of the residents had been physically or sexually abused. This halfway house was their first experience of safety—and for many, of responsibility as well. "This place saved my life," says Lynn Morozko, who sells her plasma and works at a women's shelter while earning a degree in design engineering. "A lot of people think homelessness is a type of social Darwinism," she says. "But it isn't stupid people who are homeless. It's that we hit walls that we can't get over by ourselves." Fortunately, Transitional Housing is perfecting the art of building ladders.

Hope for the Mentally Ill

One night when Todd Chimura was 15, his 13-year-old girlfriend was strangled in a Seattle park. "After that," Chimura, now 22, recalls sadly, "I stayed drunk for about five years." He took his meals at a city trash container and rotated in and out of county medical clinics. But sooner or later he would stop taking his medicine, get drunk and wake up strapped down in a hospital bed. After his sixth trip to a state mental institution, caseworkers sent him to the El Rey Treatment Facility.

The El Rey is a former Skid Row hotel, rehabbed and re-opened [in 1988] . . . as a rescue mission for homeless mentally ill people. The very design of the building reflects its treatment approach. Staff offices are scattered throughout the facility to avoid any sense of official hierarchy. Glass panels enable staff to see most areas without having to enter them. Traditionally, mental-health programs separate the most severely disturbed from others; as a patient's condition improves, he must move to a new building, new doctors, a new community. But shuttling between clinics can take its toll. "Change is really disruptive in these people's lives," says division manager Mike Nielsen. "They can't handle going to a whole new agency and dealing with new people."

The El Rey takes a "tiered approach," combining three levels of treatment on three different floors. The second floor offers "intensive" care; the third floor gives "congregate" care for people capable of some independence; the fourth floor has apartments with kitchenettes for those who are close to returning to society. The staff is realistic in its expectations: there are virtually no rules about coming and going, and though drugs and alcohol are strongly discouraged, their use is not grounds for eviction. Persuasion rather than coercion is the rule. Unless a client is unmanageable, he will never be thrown back onto the street. Says Nielsen: "El Rey is a place where some people can live indefinitely if they choose to."

TRENDS: BETTER HOMES FOR LESS[5]

Pre-fab and modular housing, once marketed mainly to resort and suburban developers, may be a ray of hope for many Americans priced out of homeownership in the 1980s. In pre-fab housing, factories manufacture and pre-assemble components—walls, stairs, floors, and ceiling panels—that are later joined together at

[5]Article by Rand Wilson, member of the United Brotherhood of Carpenters, and Mark Sommer, from *Technology Review* 93:16+ My/Je '90. Copyright © 1990 by the Association of Alumni & Alumnae of the Massachusetts Institute of Technology. Reprinted with permission.

construction sites. In modular housing, complete sections of a home arrive in the field.

Although pre-fab and modular techniques have been applied to low- and moderate-income developments around the country in recent years, no one expects them to yield a housing boom. After a decade of declining federal housing subsidies, even advocates don't claim such technology will solve the nation's housing needs.

At a site in Baltimore, Md., employees of the pioneering Rehab Work Group recently joined pre-built upper and lower sections of town houses in a project that will provide shelter for 171 low-income families. The units, shipped from Rylond Modular Homes in Northeast, Md., came complete with all interior trim details, including cabinets, smoke detectors, and bathroom and light fixtures.

The Rehab Work Group is a division of the Enterprise Foundation established by James Rouse, the developer who is famous for upscale downtown projects in Baltimore, New York, and Boston. The foundation has financed some 16,000 housing units, giving funds to some 100 nonprofit community development corporations in 27 cities and towns.

Working with the Greater Miami Neighborhoods, the foundation helped finance 11 low-income single-family houses in Opa Locka, Fla. That project introduced innovative "foam panel" technology: a factory-manufactured exterior wall that combines drywall inside the house, plywood on the outside, and electrical connections in between. Manufactured Building Systems in Opa Locka made the panels. Each home cost $32,000 to build, 20 percent less than any other housing produced in the county.

In Boston, when the Public Facilities Department (PFD) makes vacant city lots available for affordable housing, it recommends that developers hold down costs with modular or other pre-fab construction. According to a PFD study, factory construction can knock as much as 20 percent off the cost of conventional building methods in the city's overheated housing market.

Last year, the department sponsored a competition aimed at stimulating local architects and modular fabricators to develop low-cost designs. In Roxbury, winner John Sharratt is building five duplexes. His modular design is based on an identical core block that has several varieties of windows and exterior trim. It also features a garage under each unit that can be converted into additional living space. Sharratt believes that adjacent parking and an individual "look" to each house are critical to a developer's success in the inner city.

Most observers say these mass-production techniques can lower costs because they save time and materials and reduce the need for expensive on-site labor. But Gregory Beck, a senior architect in the PFD, thinks that about half the savings come from lower financing expenses. He cites "the shorter time period for relatively costly, high-risk construction loans." Financing begins after modular units arrive from a factory. In traditional stick-built construction, on the other hand, builders start paying interest with the first shipment of raw materials.

Needed: More Money

No one claims that modular or pre-fab housing is a panacea for homelessness and soaring housing costs. For one thing, Beck notes the difficulty he has attracting modular fabricators to the inner-city market. He says that transportation problems, on-site security, and opposition from construction unions all discourage modular development.

Further, Beck points out that many affordable-housing developers and construction managers have little experience with the peculiarities of modular design. Bob Santucci, a consultant to the Rehab Work Group, says he is frustrated with finding nonprofit developers capable of completing modular jobs on time.

Modular designs can also inhibit creativity. According to Sam Rappaport, who trains carpenters at Boston's non-profit Home Building Institute, "Using a modular design may lock you into a design that prevents creative local decisions."

Moreover, rehabing old housing remains much cheaper than building new units using modular or pre-built techniques. "There is a tremendous value in the older, lower-priced structures in our cities," says Santucci. "Rehabing them is much more economical than building anything new."

Pre-fab and modular housing efforts also share a number of problems with other approaches to building low-cost homes. Santucci says that too often, only unwanted land is available, so low-cost inner-city housing construction tends to be relegated to inferior building sites. That's another reason the Enterprise Foundation continues to focus its efforts on rehabing.

Finally, neither rehabing nor novel technology can address the lack of money available for affordable housing. Rouse, who headed a National Housing Task Force in 1988, has told Congress that making significant inroads into the shortage of affordable housing requires boosting federal subsidies. Yet such funds fell from almost $33 billion in 1980 to about $8 billion . . . [in 1990].

"The only way to build low-income housing is to put subsidies into it," says Helen Szablya, the Enterprise Foundation's public-relations director. Adds Santucci, "I don't think that it's a technological problem. It's a land and capital costs problem."

A NEW ENTERPRISE[6]

Imagine a United States in which one in five children will be brought up and remain in poverty, one-half of all black children will remain poor, almost half of all black teenagers will be unemployed, over seven million households will live in substandard housing, and over one million people are homeless.

Imagine a United States with thirty-four million people in poverty, where a full-time working minimum wage puts you in that category and where national educational scores have declined over the past decade. Imagine a country deemed the most violent in the Western world, one with more people per capita in overcrowded jails than any other. Imagine a country with a flourishing drug trade—the alternative economy of the inner city—and some of the most dreadful housing conditions of any industrialized nation, including the Soviet Union.

Then, picture the United States as one of the best-housed countries in the world, with new millionaires being made every day in real estate or on Wall Street. Picture one of the most affluent, productive countries in the world.

These are, of course, the same United States; the differences cited are a product of one's perspective. Between 1980 and 1984, $25 billion in disposable income changed hands from poor and middle-income Americans to the richest 20 percent of the population, according to the Urban Institute. Surely this is a trend that

[6]Article by F. Barton Harvey, deputy chairman and member of the board of trustees of the Enterprise Foundation, from *The Humanist* 49:14+ My/Je '89. Copyright © 1989 by The American Humanist Association. Reprinted with permission.

has continued. The schism between rich and poor has never been greater.

The problem of a lack of affordable housing in the United States is not only one of habitable structures but also of incomes, neighborhoods, changed attitudes, and opened opportunities. As chief executive officer of the Rouse Company, a major real estate development company, Jim Rouse saw the worlds of the rich and poor collide in urban areas and wondered why such dreadful conditions had to exist, sometimes side by side with great wealth. He asked why the creativity, ingenuity, and problem-solving capacity of the free enterprise system couldn't be applied toward the human needs of our society. Where had the government housing programs fallen short? What new efforts were necessary to combat seemingly intractable inner city problems?

The Enterprise Foundation, launched in 1982 by Jim Rouse, was inspired by his ten-year association with Jubilee Housing, a neighborhood-based organization in the Adams-Morgan section of Washington, D.C. Jubilee Housing started in 1971 at the initiative of two women from the Church of the Savior. With Jim Rouse's help, they purchased two occupied buildings with 920 code violations between them. Elevator shafts were being used as garbage dumps, and the buildings were drug distribution centers. Relying upon volunteer help, local residents, community organizing, outside pro bono assistance and fund raising, and a board of directors that represents the neighborhood, those two buildings and seven others now offer over 350 units of decent, affordable housing for very low-income residents. All nine buildings are now managed by former tenants.

Just as importantly, Jubilee Housing and its related offshoots have systematically combined housing with residents' other needs. Jubilee Jobs will place over one thousand "hard to employ" in jobs this year alone. Columbia Road Health Service, open to the neediest, serves twenty-five thousand cases a year and has helped improve the medical conditions in the neighborhood. Shelter and transitional housing for the homeless, as well as many other services, are oriented toward helping individuals who are capable of becoming self-sufficient. The changed attitudes, the harnessing of individual effort, the creative, flexible, and cost-effective use of resources, and the demonstrable positive effect on the people of the neighborhood hold hope of fashioning a national, neighborhood-based response to the massive problems facing urban areas in the United States.

The Enterprise Foundation is that national effort. It works through nonprofit, grass-roots groups serving the very poor—whom the Enterprise Foundation identifies as those earning less than $11,000 a year. Its field staff works in partnership with the groups to help them build their capacity to produce housing and provide other services. The foundation provides small grants and "linchpin loans" to tie together other public and private money for low-income housing rehabilitation and offers technical assistance and financial packaging. Enterprise's mission is to help poor people help themselves into decent housing and onto the road to self-sufficiency.

In its bottom-up approach, the Enterprise Foundation seeks to stimulate individual and local initiative, find better ways of achieving neighborhood goals, evaluate the cost and benefits of different programs, and be entrepreneurial. The neighborhood must function as a positive force in the lives of the poor for housing to be an engine of change; therefore, housing often must be coupled with many other human services.

Enterprise now works with seventy neighborhood groups in twenty-seven cities and the state of Maine. Instead of obstacles, it has found remarkable opportunities to build a new national system, linking groups through shared goals, holding up one group's solutions to another, and acting as a national clearinghouse to provide knowledge and experience.

Since its inception, the Enterprise Foundation has committed to and raised for its network groups approximately $20 million in loans and grants that have enabled construction or rehabilitation of more than three thousand units of low-income housing with a total development cost of more than $100 million. The foundation has raised $44 million from the private sector through individual contributors, corporations, foundation grants, and loans. Fund disbursement and policy are directed by a strong, distinguished board of directors which includes prominent members of the business and development community, government officials, and housing experts.

The Enterprise Foundation was also set up with a promising, long-term funding source: its wholly owned Enterprise Development Company. The development company makes its private sector contribution as it becomes profitable, pays taxes, and pays dividends back to the foundation, thereby supporting its work. The development company is a mixed-use, commercial real estate developer similar to the Rouse Company, which specializes in festival marketplaces. Its projects in Baltimore, Maryland, Battle

Creek and Flint, Michigan, Norfolk and Richmond, Virginia, and Toledo, Ohio, have generated more than four thousand new permanent jobs, fifty new minority businesses, and over $2 billion of new investments in formerly depressed downtowns. Although started with $1 million of capital from the foundation, the Enterprise Development Company is independently financed, and the foundation expects to generate $5 million to $10 million of cash flow annually by the late 1990s. Until that point, the Enterprise Foundation must support itself through fund-raising.

In formulating its approach, the Enterprise Foundation, like a well-run business, must find the best solutions given its scant resources. The foundation has found that housing rehabilitation costs too much. Middle-class systems and standards, with their attendant costs, have filtered down to low-income housing. From a nationwide study, the Enterprise Rehabilitation Work Group (RWG)—comprised of thirteen experts in housing rehabilitation and new construction—have looked at all ways of reducing costs, such as reducing room size, repairing older systems, using alternative building materials, setting up nonprofit donated materials warehouses, and eliminating unnecessary frills. Neighborhood groups affiliated with Enterprise have achieved a 20 percent reduction in housing rehabilitation costs through the efforts of RWG. In new construction, three-bedroom modular homes, built with Ryland Homes, sold for under $30,000 per house outside Columbia, Maryland, and similar designs are being used in Baltimore.

The cost of financing low-income housing rehabilitation is too high and must be reduced for viable problems to reach the very poor. The Enterprise Social Investment Corporation (ESIC) was formed in 1983 to seek out lowest-cost financing and make imaginative use of available resources for the housing programs of the network groups. ESIC actively uses the federal low-income housing tax credit and pools of benevolent loan funds from churches, businesses, and individuals. It advises states and localities on dedicated sources of funding for low-income housing, such as real estate transfer taxes or zoning bonus-linkage funds. ESIC packages federal, state, local, and private funding to make housing affordable to poor families (rents or mortgage payments around $250 a month). "Sweat equity," or payment in hours of work instead of money, home-ownership counseling, and tenant management are all used to keep costs low and individual participation high.

Finally, a housing delivery system is crucial for nonprofit development to reach a scale that can impact the size of the affordable housing problem in this country. The Enterprise Foundation is looking in a number of places—Baltimore, Cleveland, Dallas, Miami, York, Pennsylvania, and the state of Maine—to develop systems and partnerships between the public and private sectors that can become major housing production systems. The foundation has helped to create partnerships which use nonprofit developers, sponsoring neighborhood groups, and even direct development to further neighborhood development plans. In many of these cities, elements of the Enterprise Foundation have been recreated locally to cut costs, finance housing, and place people in jobs. For instance, the Cleveland Housing Network, Greater Miami-Neighborhoods, Inc., the Center for Housing Resources—Dallas, and the Maine Housing Enterprise, Inc., serve as "local intermediaries" to bring together churches, banks, foundations, nonprofit organizations, cities, and the business sector to target resources and coordinate efforts.

In the city of Chattanooga, the Enterprise Foundation's most ambitious undertaking is well underway after a year of planning. Citizens of Chattanooga, through a newly founded nonprofit organization, Chattanooga Neighborhood Enterprise, Inc. (CNE), have agreed to a $200 million program to make all housing fit and affordable within ten years. Over $2.5 million was raised privately within ninety days to staff the venture, and leading citizens, including the mayor, key businesspersons, and civic leaders, joined CNE in tackling the effort. Community-wide planning is underway, a new community bank is envisioned, locally dedicated sales taxes have been announced, state and federal assistance has been sought, and over one hundred units of housing are under construction. Chattanooga's success over the coming years can be a lighthouse to other cities that are seeking solutions to their homelessness problems.

The Enterprise Foundation's efforts, however, are a series of pilot programs in the face of the larger problem. No single effort can repair the shameful, fearful deterioration in the fabric of our neighborhoods. The 1980 census shows that 42 percent of the thirteen million families with incomes under $10,000 paid more than 50 percent of their income for rent. The statistics are even worse today. The 1985 Long-Range Planning Report of the National Association of Home Builders notes:

The housing, economic, and social problems of the nation's underclass are expected to worsen in the future as a growing segment of the population falls below the poverty line. Shortages of low-cost units will make it impossible for some households to obtain any type of housing.

The consequences of this inclusion are frightening to contemplate: homelessness, joblessness, crime, violence, and further disintegration of our cities and society.

The private sector, including the more than four hundred nonprofit organizations that have produced over ten thousand units of affordable housing, must be involved. However, this sector simply cannot replace the federal government's necessary involvement. Since 1980, the federal government has cut its housing assistance budget by two-thirds, more than any other domestic program, in the face of growing homelessness. Enterprise Foundation chairman Jim Rouse has chaired the National Housing Task Force, called for by Senators Alan Cranston and Alfonse D'Amato, which asserts that the federal government must reaffirm its commitment to "a decent suitable environment for all Americans" in a different way. The federal government should stimulate with funding the efforts of states, localities, and the private sector to live up to their community responsibilities: to creatively address the problems, to release the efforts of caring, compassionate people, and to involve self-help to the greatest extent possible.

Institutions like the Enterprise Foundation can point the way, start the process, demonstrate models that work, and return hope and action to the poor. By showing what can be accomplished, it can raise new convictions about the cities and generate a new state of discontent with the way poor people are living and how neighborhoods are deteriorating. It offers a call to action that we all need to hear.

BIBLIOGRAPHY

An asterisk (*) preceding a reference indicates that the material or part of it has been reprinted in this book.

BOOKS AND PAMPHLETS

Barak, Gregg. Gimme shelter. A social history of homelessness in contemporary America. Praeger Publishers. '91.

Bard, Marjorie. Shadow women: Homeless women's survival stories. Sheed & Ward. '90.

Erikson, Jon, & Wilhelm, Charles, eds. Housing the homeless. The Center for Urban Policy Research. '86.

Evans, Michael, A., ed. Homeless in America. Acropolis Books Ltd. '88.

Fagan, Margaret. The fight against homelessness. Franklin Watts. '90.

Farnsworth, Philip S., and Baker, Vernon G. Under the bridge. Farnsworth & Baker. '88.

Foster, Carol D., et al., eds. Homeless: How could it happen here? Information Plus Services. '89.

Fowler, Tom, et al., eds., Out of the rain. Strawberry Hill Press. '88.

Friedrichs, Juergen, ed. Affordable housing & the homeless. Walter De Gruyter. '88.

Giamo, Benedict. On the Bowery: Confronting homelessness in America. University of Iowa Press. '89.

Gorder, Cheryl. Homeless! Without addresses in America. Blue Bird Publishers. '88.

Grady, Duane. Helping the homeless. Bretheren Press. '88.

Hirsch, Kathleen. Songs from the alley. Doubleday. '90.

Hoch, Charles, & Slayton, Robert A. New homeless and old: Community & the skid row hotel. Temple University Press. '90.

Hombs, Mary Ellen. American homelessness: A reference handbook. ABC-Clio. '90.

Hombs, Mary Ellen, & Snyder, Mitch. Homelessness in America: A forced march to nowhere, 2nd. ed. The Committee for Creative Non-Violence. '83.

Hope, Marjorie, & Young, James. The faces of homelessness. Free Press. '86.

Hubbard, Jim. American Refugees. University of Minnesota Press. '91.

Hyde, Margaret. The homeless: Profiling the problem. Enslow Publishers. '89.

Isaac, Rael Jean & Armat, Virginia. Madness in the streets. The Free Press. '90.

Johnson, Joan J. Kids without homes. Franklin Watts. '91.

Jones, Billy E., ed. Treating the homeless: Urban psychiatry's challenge. UMI Research Press. '85.

Killilea, William S. In.Dig.Na.Tion: A homeless story. Vantage. '89.

Kosof, Anna. Homeless in America. Franklin Watts. '88.

Kozol, Jonathan. Rachel & her children: Homeless families in America. Fawcett. '88.

Lang, Michael H. Homelessness amid affluence: Structure & paradox in the American political economy. Greenwood Press. '89.

McDaniel, Judith. Sanctuary, a journey. Firebrand Books. '87.

Momeni, Jamshid A., ed. Homelessness in the United States, 2 vol. Greenwood Press. '89.

O'Connor, Karen. Homeless Children. Lucent Books. '89.

O'Neill, Terry. The homeless: Distinguishing between fact & opinion. Greenhaven Press. '90.

Orr, Lisa, ed. The homeless: Opposing viewpoints. Greenhaven Press. '90.

Pearce, Diana M. The invisible homeless: Women & children. The Institute of Women's Policy Research. '88.

Redburn, F. Stevens, & Buss, Terry F. Responding to America's homelessness: Public policy alternatives. Greenwood Press. '86.

Resener, Carl R. Crisis in the streets. Broadman Press. '88.

Ringheim, Karin. At risk of homelessness: The roles of income and rent. Greenwood Press. '90.

Robertson, M. J., & Greenblatt, M., eds. Homelessness: The national perspective. Plenum Publishing Corp. '91.

Ropers, Richard H. The invisible homeless: A new urban ecology. Human Sciences Press. '88.

Rossi, Peter H. Down & out in America: The origins of homelessness. The University of Chicago Press. '89.

Rousseau, Ann Marie, & Shulman, Alix K. Shopping bag ladies: Homeless women speak about their lives. The Pilgrim Press. '82.

Stavsky, Lois, & Mozeson, J. E. The place I call home: The faces and voices of homeless teens. Shapolsky Publishers. '90.

Stoner, Madeleine R. Inventing a non-homeless future: A public policy agenda for preventing homelessness. Peter Lang Publishing. '89.

Susko, Michael A., ed. Cry of the invisible: Writings from the homeless & survivors of psychiatric hospitals. Conservatory. '91.

Thorman, George. Homeless Families. Charles C. Thomas. '88.

Timmer, Doug A., & Eitzen, D. Stanley. The homeless in America. Westview Press. '91.

Torrey, E. Fuller. Nowhere to go: The tragic odyssey of the homeless mentally ill. HarperCollins. '89.

U.S. House of Representatives. Select Committee on Children, Youth, & Families. The crisis in homelessness: Effects on children and families. U.S. Government Printing Office. '87.

Watson, Sophie, & Austerberry, Helen. Housing & homelessness: A feminist perspective. Routledge & Kegan Paul. '86.

Wright, James D. Address unknown: The homeless in America. Aldine de Gruyter. '89.

ADDITIONAL PERIODICAL ARTICLES WITH ABSTRACTS

For those who wish to read more widely on the subject of the homeless, this section contains abstracts of additional articles that bear on the topic. Readers who require a comprehensive list of materials are advised to consult the *Readers' Guide to Periodical Literature* and other Wilson indexes.

The prejudice against men. P. Marin. *The Nation* 253:46–8+ Jl 8 '91

Homelessness is mainly a problem that afflicts single adult men. For numerous reasons linked to prejudice, more men than women end up homeless on America's streets. The U.S. welfare system was designed primarily to aid women and children, not men. At the root of the problem is society's belief that if men cannot take care of themselves and others, they are unworthy of help. Men who cannot find work are thought to be superfluous and dangerous, and society feels compelled to banish them from view. Homeless men often feel helpless, vulnerable, and isolated. Most of them seem to have been deprived of the connection, support, and sustenance that would enable them to find and keep places in the social order, and they feel betrayed by society. Confronting the root causes of homelessness and trying to amend the situation will remain utopian notions until society confronts its prejudices and oppressive practices in relation to men in general and homeless men in particular.

Shantytown. J. Lardner. *The New Yorker* 67:67–76 Jl 1 '91

The Hill, a makeshift squatter settlement alongside the Manhattan Bridge, may be the most permanent of the shantytowns that have sprung up in New York in recent years. About 20 people live on the Hill, most of whom have already experienced other forms of homelessness such as living in shelters or on the street. They insist on a degree of autonomy and anonymity not to be found in a city shelter, but they also have a sense of permanence and community. Most residents work hard at scavenging abandoned furniture and appliances, and many of them have provided their huts with electricity siphoned from nearby lampposts. The Hill's residents sometimes fight among themselves, but they tend to look out for one another and have tried to adopt some basic rules of sanitation, discipline, and civility. Several residents of the Hill are profiled.

New York's new ghettos. C. J. Vergara. *The Nation* 252:804–6+ Je 17 '91

New York City's ambitious project for addressing homelessness is creating new ghettos for the poor. By locating 9 of its 13 new shelters in some of the city's most depressed, drug ridden, and violent communities, the city has contained and concentrated its weakest and neediest people. If these people are not residents of a new shelter, then they live in a neighboring old shelter, group home, or correctional institution or frequent nearby drug treatment centers, methadone clinics, or soup kitchens. Five of the new communities are in the South Bronx, the new homeless capital; three are in a section of northeast Brooklyn; and one is in Manhattan. New fair share rules designed to promote the even distribution of such facilities among the city's rich and poor sections came into effect too late to prevent the creation of homeless communities. These communities need to be dismantled, regardless of the rules, because they contribute to dependency, illness, and delinquency.

Myths about the homeless. R. J. Bidinotto. *Reader's Digest* 138:98–103 Je '91

The truth about homelessness in the United States has been shrouded in fallacies and misrepresentations. Reports by the media, politicians, and homeless advocacy groups assert that homeless people number in the millions, that many are working people who got unlucky, and that families account for the fastest growing segment of the homeless population. Studies reveal that this information is erroneous. In reality, the total number of homeless is only a fraction of the millions reported. In addition, it is rare to find a homeless family consisting of a husband and wife with children in tow; most of the chronically homeless are single or unattached men, many of whom abuse alcohol or drugs or suffer from a mental health problem. Although it is not easy to get the homeless off the streets, it can be done if supervised care for the mentally incapacitated is mandated, if vagrancy laws are enacted and enforced, and if assistance is tied to responsible behavior.

Nightmare on Jane Street. J. Kasindorf. *New York* 23:30–8 S 17 '90

Homeless man Bill Emerson has been charged with the July 30 murder of advertising executive John Reisenbach in New York City's Greenwich Village. Reisenbach was shot three times as he spoke on a pay telephone near his home on Jane Street. At the eastern end of the street, many homeless people live in several parks, and at the western end, transvestite prostitutes, pimps, and crack dealers have encroached on the neighborhood. Emerson is reportedly a bright but emotionally troubled man whose life has been derailed by alcohol and cocaine. He was charged with the murder after a transvestite named Porsche and a homeless person named Larry said that he was responsible. Larry did not see the murder but says that Emerson told him he had committed it. Porsche confuses some times and places in his story. Emerson has pleaded not guilty and is now awaiting trial at Rikers Island.

The kindness of strangers. F. Chideya. *Newsweek* 116:48 Ag 13 '90

From Boston to San Francisco, entrepreneurs are establishing newspapers and magazines that are sold by the homeless. The owners see themselves as providing the homeless with the opportunity to help themselves. In New York, for example, homeless vendors earn an average of $90 per day by buying copies of *Street News* for $0.30 and reselling them for $0.75. Some critics, however, believe that the homeless are being exploited as cheap labor, and the owners themselves fear that the vendors could fall victim to a public backlash against the homeless.

Good news for the homeless. M. E. Johnson and S. Brewer. *New Choices for the Best Years* 30:9 Jl '90

Street News, a biweekly newspaper published in New York City, is helping homeless people get off the streets. The newspaper's mission is to provide work for some of the city's 70,000 homeless people. Since the paper's initial publication in December, several hundred vendors have earned enough money to rent their own apartments. Regional editions of the paper are planned for San Francisco and Washington, D.C.

Blues for the homeless. L. Birnbaum. *Down Beat* 57:23–5 Ag '90

Drummer Art Blakey, keyboardist and guitarist Dr. John, and horn player David Newman have teamed up to produce *Bluesiana Triangle* (Windham

Hill), a benefit album for the National Coalition for the Homeless. The recording is an extraordinary meeting of musical minds. Aided by bassist Essiet Okon Essiet and percussionist Joe Bonadio, the three musicians create free-spirited tunes with a strong spiritual tone. Highlights of the album are the groove-laden "Need to Be Loved," the bluesy "One Way Ticket," the vintage ballad "For All We Know," and the spine-chilling "When the Saints Go Marchin' In."

Beyond shelter for the homeless. M. Bauerlein. *The Progressive* 54:12 S '90

Members of the aggressive Minneapolis activist group Up and Out of Poverty Now! have been squatting in vacant houses owned by the Department of Housing and Urban Development (HUD). The activists say that they are tired of waiting for HUD to fulfill its promise that 10 percent of HUD homes would be turned over to groups working for low-income housing. That would mean about 80 properties in Minnesota, but only 17 have been leased so far. Although HUD officials appear unimpressed with the group's actions, local officials have offered to cooperate with the activists, a move that reflects the growing dissatisfaction with federal low-income-housing policy among local officials in Minneapolis and elsewhere. Minneapolis officials are now considering a housing program similar to Philadelphia's Dignity Housing.

Tent City blues. S. Ferguson. *Mother Jones* 15:29–30 S/O '90

Renaldo Casanova, who leads the Tent City organization of homeless people in New York City, represents a new breed of homeless activists who are working to help themselves in ways that service providers or would-be advocates can't. Casanova's path toward self empowerment has included leading the Tent City encampment in Tompkins Square Park, fighting off successive police raids, camping out in front of the United Nations, and traveling throughout America as an organizer for the National Union of the Homeless. He and many other homeless activists have challenged both conservatives' efforts to stereotype the homeless and the often patronizing and self fulfilling efforts of liberal advocates to either serve or "reform" the homeless. The informal network of homeless activists now includes the United Homeless Organization in Manhattan, Dignity Housing in Philadelphia and Oakland, and the Homeless Outreach Program in Los Angeles.

Us vs. them: America's growing frustration with the homeless. S. Ferguson. *Utne Reader* 50–5 S/O '90

An article excerpted from an April 16, 1990, Pacific News Service report. A class war is brewing between angry homeless people and other citizens.

Antagonism toward the homeless is rising, which has helped encourage urban efforts to cut aid to the homeless and place new restrictions on them. One reason for the backlash is the overwhelming numbers of indigents. Another is that the prevailing stereotype of the homeless person as a meek skid row bum has been replaced by the image of angry young African-American and Hispanic men who may demand money with a sense of entitlement that passersby find enraging. Increasingly, angry homeless people have begun joining forces, demanding political recognition and fighting back when they don't get it.

School + home = a program for educating homeless students. M.-L. González. *Phi Delta Kappan* 71:785–7 Je '90

City Park School in Dallas, Texas, is an inner-city school that has achieved remarkable success in serving homeless students. The school was selected as 1 of 15 exemplary programs providing education for homeless children in the United States. Its success stems from its procedures to orient its students, the coordination of effort among its staff, and the involvement of community groups. Homeless students are not differentiated from other students at City Park but are "accepted" into the school with the help of fellow students, staff, and faculty. The academic and psychosocial progress of homeless students is closely monitored, and the community helps out with financial and volunteer support.

Whither the homeless? *National Review* 43:18 My 13 '91

Only a small percentage of homeless people are homeless because of economic conditions. Building codes, zoning laws, rent regulations, and tax policies have prevented the private sector from providing adequate low cost housing. In addition, government efforts on behalf of the homeless are stymied. In New York and Boston, for example, where rent is controlled, there are too few affordable apartments available to house Section 8 recipients, and between 30 and 60 percent of the vouchers are returned unspent to housing authorities. In Chicago, on the other hand, where rents are not controlled, landlords seek Section 8 recipients. In the 1980s, the United States learned to let the market alone to remedy the energy shortage; in the 1990s, that lesson may be applied to housing.

The ACLU and economic rights. S. Walker. *Society* 28:14–16 Ja/F '91

Part of a special section on the American Civil Liberties Union (ACLU). The ACLU's policies regarding the poor and the homeless rest on the principles of equal protection and due process. The organization does not, as some of its critics have suggested, assert an absolute right to shelter or impose an obligation on the U.S. government to provide shelter. The seven suits that were recently brought by the Southern California ACLU on behalf of the homeless were not based on new concepts of economic rights; they were based on well-established principles of law. This explains why the California affiliate, in concert with other organizations, won all of the cases.

Home is where the art is. A. Atkins. *New Choices for the Best Years* 31:60–3 F '91

Los Angeles sculptor Jacqueline Dreager has established the Homeless Outreach Program to teach art to the city's homeless people. After being selected as artist-in-residence by Los Angeles Contemporary Exhibitions, Dreager began holding art classes in a storefront studio. She provides her students with art supplies and inspiration to create everything from paintings to sculpture. Other artists have donated supplies and materials, and the studio has received a bank of lockers, which are essential for homeless people who have no place to store their possessions. The class, which has a core group of four people and other students who drift in and out on a weekly basis, is providing the homeless with a way to become productive citizens. Last September, Dreager's students held their first exhibit at the Gene Sinser Gallery.

The big empty. D. Frey. *Rolling Stone* p77–8+ Ap 18 '91

Stamford, Connecticut, has transformed itself into a corporate powerhouse, but it has neglected the needs of its poorest citizens. The city has attracted more than two dozen New York corporations, including GTE, Xerox, Champion, and Olin, and the metropolitan area now has the third largest concentration of *Fortune* 500 headquarters in the country. Meanwhile, the city's homeless population has grown, and the places where the homeless are welcome continue to dwindle. One of the city's homeless victims was Teresa Watson, who arrived in Stamford eight years ago looking for friends she never found. Watson was planning to leave the city with the help of a social worker who had promised to buy her a bus ticket. Before she could make her escape, however, she was murdered by two other homeless people. Stamford quickly forgot the incident as it focused on issues relating to the city's financial health.

Rock in a hard place. T. J. Meyer. *Seventeen* 49:130–3 N '90

A strong heavy metal scene has helped make Los Angeles the leading destination for teenage runaways. More than 10,000 teenagers flock to the city each year in response to success stories about such groups as Mötley Crüe, Guns n' Roses, and Poison. The scene is highly competitive, however, with as many as 2,000 heavy metal bands fighting for recognition and club dates. These bands vie for the attention of about 20 record companies, each of which signs only three new metal groups a year. Many teenagers who come to Los Angeles with visions of overnight success instead end up living in shelters or abandoned buildings, while others become easy prey for pimps and pornographers.

Shrugging off the homeless. P. Painton *Time* 135:14–16 Ap 16 '90

New Yorkers are growing increasingly impatient with panhandlers. The sour mood toward the homeless has been reflected in newspaper cartoons, dinner conversations, and official campaigns to move the city's vagrants out of subway, bus, and train stations. According to Robert Kiley, chairman of the Metropolitan Transportation Authority, people who would have merely walked away a year ago are now snapping back at aggressive panhandlers. In their relations with the public, the homeless may be harmed by the perception that they are a permanent fixture of urban life. Another problem is that the term homeless groups together not only the destitute in need of shelter but also AIDS victims, the mentally ill, drug and alcohol abusers, and street predators of all kinds.

Homeless bond. R. Rowan. *People Weekly* 33:70–6+ Mr 5 '90

A reporter who spent two weeks posing as a homeless man on the streets of New York City describes his encounters with homeless people, the way he was treated by the public and the police, and his experiences in drop-in centers, soup kitchens, and other places frequented by the homeless. The worst part of being homeless, he found, was the dehumanizing loss of dignity.

Would they be better off in a home? L. Schiff. *National Review* 42:33–5 Mr 5 '90

Homelessness would be less of a problem if the mental health system stopped promoting the myth that a large percentage of the homeless are mentally ill and if the government stopped making homelessness a viable alternative to middle-class living. Although some homeless people have severe mental problems, the vast majority do not. Many homeless people are diagnosed as mentally ill so that state-run mental hospitals, whose budgets are predicated upon the expenditure of all monies for the present year, can maintain their budgets at high levels. Most homeless people are minorities from lower-income areas who see homeless shelters as better alternatives to the vicious neighborhoods from which they come. The only real solution to homelessness is to promote sound moral and economic values in the lower class.

New shapes in shelters. J. Adler. *Newsweek* 115:38–9 Ja 1 '90

Architects and planners are designing shelters for the homeless that resemble modern apartments. Some of the better new shelters, like the St.
Vincent de Paul/Joan Kroc Center in San Diego, have spacious, private
rooms and such amenities as underground parking for volunteers. The
rise of a homeless class of women and children has contributed to the
demands for space and privacy.

The homeless at Christmas. M. Novak. *Forbes* 144:70 D 25 '89

As Peter Rossi points out in *Down and Out in America: The Origins of Homelessness*, the number of homeless people in the United States has been
wildly exaggerated. On any one night, he has found, the homeless
number only about 300,000, or 1 American out of 1,000. Given that the
number of homeless people is so small, the homeless problem clearly is
not insuperable. The most practical people in the country should be able
to come up with a solution, which should involve the profit motive, market forces, and some kind of substitute for the cheap flophouses of by-
gone days.

Kemp OKs use of vacant apartments for homeless. *Jet* 77:52 N
27 '89

Jack Kemp, secretary of the Department of Housing and Urban Development, has changed a previous requirement in order to give the Chicago
Housing Authority (CHA) permission to rent some of the city's vacant
apartments to homeless people this winter. Prior to the change, CHA
apartments were available only to low-income families, senior citizens, and
handicapped persons. According to CHA chairman Vincent Lane, approximately 400 to 600 apartments will be rented to the homeless.

Helping them help themselves. L. Whitaker. *Time* 135:56 F 26
'90

A new nonprofit publication called *Street News* is designed to help the
homeless earn money instead of begging for it. *Street News* founder and
editor in chief Hutchinson Persons, who created the paper with borrowed
money and donations, says that nearly 1,000 homeless and near homeless
people have sold more than 1 million copies in New York City since the
first issue debuted four months ago. Five additional cities are targeted for
distribution by year's end. The salespeople pay approximately $0.25 per
paper and sell them for $0.75, pocketing the difference. An extra nickel
for every paper sold is deposited in a savings account set aside for rent.
The monthly publication consists largely of pieces written by celebrities
and business executives, but the most interesting pieces are the prose and

poems contributed by homeless people. Some observers are critical of the operation, arguing that the homeless need a host of services rather than just temporary work opportunities.

Homeless in poor mental, physical health. *Science News* 136:302 N 4 '89

Three studies demonstrate the extent to which homeless people suffer from serious health problems. In the October 13 issue of the *Journal of the American Medical Association,* Lillian Gelberg of UCLA's Division of Family Medicine and Lawrence S. Linn report that of the 529 homeless people whom they examined, two-thirds had physical symptoms that required immediate medical care. William R. Breakey and Pamela J. Fischer of the Johns Hopkins University School of Medicine in Baltimore found similar problems in 528 homeless men and women interviewed at missions, shelters, and jails. They reported their findings in the September 8 issue of the *Journal of the American Medical Association.* In a study of 55 homeless people described in the September-October issue of *Public Health Reports,* Elisabeth Luder of New York City's Mount Sinai School of Medicine notes that nutritionally inadequate diets may contribute to homeless adults' poor health.

Despair: the plight of our homeless. J. Ambrose and G. White. *USA Today (Periodical)* 118:54–65 Mr '90

A major photographic exhibition depicting the plight of America's homeless people is touring U.S. cities. The purpose of the exhibit is to help awaken Americans to the complex and diverse causes of homelessness and to offer proof that families compose the fastest growing segment of the homeless population. Community organizations have launched several educational, fund raising, and public awareness events in coordination with the exhibit, which is a joint effort of the National Mental Health Association and Families of the Homeless. Several photographs from the exhibit are reproduced.

Educating homeless children. A. S. Wells. *The Education Digest* 55:30–2 Ap '90

An article condensed from *ERIC Clearinghouse on Urban Education Digest,* No. 52, 1989. The education of homeless children creates serious problems for already overburdened urban school administrators and teachers. Under a 1987 federal law, schools can no longer deny access to homeless students who lack proof of residency and must waive guardianship rules for homeless students living with foster parents or nonparental relatives. Schools are also subject to statewide educational plans developed by state officials in accordance with the same law. The most common problems associated with educating homeless children and the programs favored by local educators to meet the children's needs are discussed.

Schools for the homeless. K. R. Moyer. *The Education Digest* 55:48–50 F '90

An article condensed from the Spring 1989 issue of *State Education Leader.* In response to the disturbing number of homeless children in the United States who do not attend school regularly or at all, many special programs and schools are emerging to make certain that these children do not miss out on an education. According to the National Coalition for the Homeless, 500,000 to 750,000 children in the United States are homeless, and 57 percent of them do not attend school regularly. A survey by the U.S. Conference of Mayors concluded that 43 percent of homeless children don't attend school at all. In such cities as Santa Clara, California; Salt Lake City, Utah; and Tacoma, Washington, schools for homeless children are being set up at homeless family shelters. A program adopted by the New York Board of Regents and the City of Boston allows homeless parents to choose the schools that their children attend.

Educating children of the homeless. E. A. Eddowes and J. R. Hranitz. *The Education Digest* 55:15–17 O '89

An article condensed from the summer issue of *Childhood Education.* Homeless children face a host of problems, but none is more critical than the struggle to receive a decent education. Homeless parents face considerable difficulties enrolling their children in school. Those who are enrolled may have to travel long distances, and they often encounter harassment, rejection, and academic difficulty. Many drop out of school as a result. To improve the situation, more effective lines of communication must be created between schools and service-providing agencies, day care programs and schools must be made more accessible to the homeless, and individualized educational programs must receive more support.

Address unknown: homelessness in contemporary America. J. D. Wright. *Society* 26:45–53 S/O '89

Part of a special section on social and economic policy for the 1990s. The number of homeless people in American cities has grown significantly in the past decade. Based on statistics for Chicago, an estimated 800,000 Americans are homeless on any given night, while the annual homeless population of the nation is on the order of 1,500,000. Despite popular stereotypes, only a minority of homeless people are mentally ill, chronic alcoholics, recipients of government benefit programs, or homeless by choice. The rise in homelessness can be understood as an increasing shortage of low-income housing, caused in part by the influx of the mid-

dle class into central cities. The federal government is unlikely to spend
the funds needed to solve the problem of homelessness. The coming
decade will instead see a focus on improving the lives of homeless people.

How not to help the homeless. *U.S. News & World Report* 107:29
Ag 28–S 4 '89

The McKinney Act, enacted in 1987, was supposed to provide a painless
solution to the homelessness problem, but it has not worked as well as was
hoped. The act mandates that the federal government turn over thousands of empty surplus buildings to homeless advocates for use as kitchens, health clinics, and shelters. Compliance with the act has been slow,
despite a U.S. court order demanding that the government make more
property available. The problem stems partly from the scandal plaguing
the Department of Housing and Urban Development (HUD), as well as
from bureaucratic gamesmanship. In addition, the act gives HUD no
authority to force other agencies to transfer surplus property to the
homeless.

Homeless rights, community wrongs. J. Leo. *U.S. News & World
Report* 107:56 Jl 24 '89

The homeless deserve aid and compassion, but they should not be allowed
to destabilize communities. Almost all programs aimed at the homeless
have been produced by the Left, which frames the homelessness issue as a
clash between a heartless government and beleaguered victims. The
homeless are thus allowed to camp in parks, making these areas unusable
by other members of the community and turning them into breeding
grounds for crimes. Efforts to deal with the problem are often obstructed
by liberals. In New York City, for instance, proposed regulations against
panhandling in parks and lying down on park benches for more than two
hours were attacked. Unless liberal leaders consider community issues in
their proposals for the homeless, the problems will not be solved.

Give the homeless a chance. K. R. Smith. *Christianity Today* 33:8 Jl
14 '89

Charitable efforts by individuals and groups are insufficient to stem the
tide of homelessness caused by poorly conceived government policies of
the 1970s and 1980s. Many of the homeless are mentally ill people who
were deinstitutionalized in the 1970s and left to fend for themselves.
Others are poor people who are victims of the Reagan administration's
deep cuts in funding for low-income housing. The best way to alleviate
homelessness is to promote affordable housing through direct action and
lobbying.

Middle America: priced out of house and home. K. S. Dieg-mueller. *Current (Washington, D.C.)* 314:16–21 Jl/Ag '89

An article reprinted from the March 13, 1989, issue of *Insight.* The Bush administration is expected to create a new national housing program that will pay particular attention to the problems of low-income families, the homeless, and first-time home buyers. As housing prices rise, more young couples remain in rental units, which increases competition for these spaces, drives up rents, and squeezes out moderate- and low-income households. Low-income housing has also been reduced by demolition, condo conversion, the Reagan-era slashing of the Department of Housing and Urban Development's budget, and developers' tendency to concentrate on building higher-end units. It is estimated that the United States will need an additional 8 million low-income units by the year 2000. As the government works to create more housing, it must also summon the resources to rehabilitate existing low-income units and alleviate the crime associated with them.

What we can do about the homeless. C. Whitaker. *Ebony* 44:96+ Je '89

More than 60 percent of homeless families today are black, and most of these are headed by a single mother who has small children. The National Coalition for the Homeless reports that there are close to 3 million homeless Americans, about 60 percent of whom live on some form of public assistance. People who want to help the homeless should get to know them personally by volunteering at shelters. They can also lobby politicians at the local and national level to provide low-income housing.

Homeless need more than shelter. *USA Today (Periodical)* 117:8 My '89

Social relationships are as important as shelter to the homeless, according to a study conducted for the University of Southern California's Los Angeles Homelessness Project. Jennifer Wolch, an associate professor in the School of Urban and Regional Planning, says that homelessness typically occurs in tandem with the collapse of a person's social network. Because the interpersonal relationships within social networks support identity and self esteem, homelessness tends to become self perpetuating unless social networks are rebuilt.

How to sabotage the homeless. J. Mehrten. *Conservative Digest* 15:6–7+ My/Je '89

Homeless Americans have become the subject of great concern both in and out of government, yet government persists in a course of action that can only hurt the homeless. The great surge in homeless people in recent years is due largely to court and policy decisions authorizing the release of large numbers of the institutionalized insane. A number of admirable efforts to help homeless people have been launched by church groups, but government has made their situation worse by imposing stifling regulations on the construction of the low-cost housing that they need. If legislators really care about those who cannot afford decent housing, as they claim to, they should push for deregulation of the home-building industry.

Mad Housers help homeless. L. S. Bates. *The Progressive* 53:15 My '89

Atlanta's Mad Housers, a group of people dedicated to building shelters for the homeless, have constructed more than five dozen solidly built wooden huts on public land. The huts, which measure 48 square feet, lack heating and plumbing but have a lock on the door and carpeting on the walls for insulation. The Mad Housers salvage materials from various sources and, according to cofounder Brian Pinkle, can sometimes build huts for as little as $40. Although a few huts have been removed or burned, police in Atlanta generally leave them alone. The group has won awards, gained unofficial acceptance, and seen its efforts imitated elsewhere. The Mad Housers have also received a grant from the city to build two bungalows that will serve as low-rent transitional housing. Cofounder Mike Connor would like the bungalow effort to serve as a prototype for public-private partnerships.

The unhealthy homeless. *The Futurist* 23:56-7 Jl/Ag '89

Homeless people are more susceptible to illnesses and have less access to health care than other people, according to the report *Homelessness, Health, and Human Needs*. People living on the street or in shelters are more apt to suffer from poor circulation, skin diseases, tuberculosis, and dental disease. They are also more likely to suffer physical trauma, as they are often the victims of violent crime. Even is they are able to receive treatment, their living situation often makes it impossible to follow doctors' instructions for getting bed rest, eating a special diet, or following a medication schedule. The homeless are also plagued by alcohol-related illnesses and mental disorders.

The dynamics of homelessness. *Children Today* 18:2-3 My/Je '89

Homelessness, Health, and Human Needs, a study published by the Committee on Health Care for Homeless People of the National Academy of Sciences, documents the plight of the homeless in 11 major cities and impoverished rural areas in several states. Committee members who conducted the study found that families with young children constitute the fastest growing component of the homeless population, that homeless shelters provide unsafe and unsanitary living conditions, and that homeless people suffer more acute and chronic illnesses and health problems than the general population. The study recommends coordinated efforts to address housing, income maintenance, and deinstitutionalization plans; the use of Emergency Assistance program funds to prevent homelessness; and enhanced federal support for outreach programs and programs aimed at children and mothers.

A sea of stars. A. Ferguson. *National Review* 41:26 N 10 '89

In the early 1980s, the "celebrity community" was a vast network of left-wing stars who would turn out to demonstrate for a variety of causes. At that time, the network was so large that demonstration organizers could select only top stars. Community interest in celebrities has dropped off, however, and organizers must make do with whatever celebrities are available. At the recent "Housing Now" event in Washington, D.C., guests paid $150 to attend a cocktail party where 250 celebrities were expected to be in attendance. A plane from Los Angeles carrying most of the celebrities was late, and many guests were disappointed. The day after the cocktail party, an appearance by Jesse Jackson at a celebrity breakfast for the homeless caused a stir, but most of the other celebrities were minor personalities who went largely unnoticed.

Speaking out for a place to call home. J. Park. *People Weekly* 32:40–3 O 23 '89

An estimated 40,000 demonstrators led by an array of celebrities rallied at the U.S. capitol this month to protest repeated cuts in the federal housing budget. Under a banner that read "Housing Now," a variety of groups joined several hundred homeless people, some of whom had walked from distant states for the demonstration.

Behind the housing crisis: private-sector forces, not Reagan, killed off affordable rentals. D. Whitman. *U.S. News & World Report* 107:28+ O 16 '89

Contrary to popular belief, the Reagan administration is not responsible for the current housing crisis. The low-income housing squeeze is primarily the result of the disintegration of the private, unsubsidized rental market. The urban renaissance of the 1980s has proved to be a disaster for the urban poor, as buildings in poor condition are renovated for wealthy tenants. High interest rates, restrictive building and land-use codes, abandonment, and arson have exacerbated the problem. The theory that Reagan's cuts in the HUD budget contributed to the crisis is misleading. In fact, appropriations from earlier decades increased spending on subsidized housing from $8.3 billion in 1980 to $16.1 billion in 1988. The problem can be alleviated if efforts are made to improve the private housing market.

Modern dancers reach out to prisoners and to homeless men. R. Johnson. *Dance Magazine* 63:15 S '89

The experiences of two modern dance companies that recently performed for audiences on the margins of society illustrate the difficulties and benefits of the "dance outreach" phenomenon of the 1980s. Bill T. Jones/Arnie Zane & Company appeared at the Men's House of Detention on Riker's Island at the invitation of the Department of Corrections. The dancers performed pieces with themes chosen to correspond with inmates' lives but were heckled by the audience throughout the show. Johari Briggs, executive director of the troupe, angrily exhorted the prisoners to remember their humanity. Inmates protested that the dances had not been explained to them. Diane Jacobowitz's dance company went to the Atlantic Avenue Armory, a Brooklyn shelter for homeless men, and performed dances exploring mortality and failed communication. The performers were enthusiastically received.

Before birth control. L. George. *American Health* 8:114–15 Jl/Ag '89

Historian John Boswell's *The Kindness of Strangers: The Abandonment of Children in Western Europe from Late Antiquity to the Renaissance* reveals that, until as late as the 18th century, it was common for European parents to abandon their unwanted children. They left their children in public places in the hope that strangers would adopt them as their own. Boswell maintains that the system worked well until the establishment of foundling homes in the 14th century. Disease became common in these institutions, and abandonment usually meant death. Boswell's book reveals that the problem of finding a civilized way to deal with homeless children transcends time.

Lost youth. R. Coles. *Vogue* 179:186–9 Jl '89

Hundreds of thousands of school-age children in the United States are homeless, usually because their families have been the victims of bad luck. Many of these children feel radically uprooted and psychologically adrift, a feeling that can profoundly undermine their self respect. The writer, a pediatrician and child psychologist, discusses his interviews with homeless children.

The homeless woman with two homes. G. Talese. *New York* 22:40–2 O 30 '89

The writer describes his encounter with a homeless woman whom he spotted on the streets of New York City. He learned that she had left her friends and family in Queens, but she gave no reason for choosing to live on the streets.

One point of light. D. Finkel. *Esquire* 112:123–8+ O '89

Sheila Braun of Honesdale, Pennsylvania, attempted to help Martha Davis, a homeless woman from New York City, start a new life, but the matchup ended in failure. Braun, a deeply religious woman, read an account of the birth of Davis's sixth child, which took place in a midtown Manhattan subway station, and offered Davis a home. Davis moved into the small house that Braun shares with her four children. Tensions eventually arose, and Davis never felt comfortable in the small town. She soon returned to New York, where she ended up on the streets again.